Studying Literary Theory

An introduction

SECOND EDITION

Roger Webster
Professor of Literary Studies
Liverpool John Moores University

ARNOLD

A member of the Hodder Headline Group
LONDON

First published in Great Britain 1990
Second edition published 1996, reprinted 2001 by
Arnold, a member of the Hodder Headline Group,
338 Euston Road, London NW1 3BH

© 1990 and 1996 Roger Webster

British Library Cataloguing in Publication Data
A catalogue entry for this book is available from the British Library

Library of Congress Cataloging-in-Publication Data
Webster, Roger, 1950-
Studying literary theory : an introduction / Roger Webster.—2nd ed.
    p.   cm.
Includes bibliographical references and index.
ISBN 0-340-58499-8
1. Criticism—Study and teaching. I. Title.
PN86.W35 1995
801'.95'07—dc20   95-31305

ISBN 0 340 58499 8

Typeset in 10/12 Times by York House Typographic Ltd, London
Printed and bound in India by Replika Press Pvt. Ltd., 100% EOU,
Delhi-110 040

Contents

Preface

This book is intended as a basic *introduction* to literary theory, and I have tried to introduce some of the main theoretical areas and debates which might be relevant to literary studies today. Clearly in a book of this kind there is a tension between overall coverage and the depth of discussion of particular areas, and inevitably there are shortcomings in both dimensions; I have though tried to indicate useful further reading wherever relevant and I hope this book acts as a stimulus to more detailed consideration of aspects of literary theory.

This new second edition builds on the previous edition in several ways. First it offers a fuller introduction to a wider range of literary theories, including poststructuralism, postmodernism, New Historicism, postcolonial theory, and theories of sexual identity. Secondly, there are more extended discussions of some areas of literary theory previously introduced together with the use of additional illustrative material where appropriate to indicate how aspects of theory might be applied to various texts. The section on further reading has also been updated.

Throughout the book I have related the various theories discussed to a range of literary texts; I have tried to select representative texts which should be familiar to readers or which are readily accessible, and have used them repeatedly where possible so that some continuity may result. Obviously though the theoretical arguments can be applied to much wider reading and I hope that other examples will come to mind or that the theories will be applied to other texts.

I hope this book will be helpful to students of literature coming to literary theory for the first time, in particular undergraduates; it may also be of interest to sixth-form students and more general readers. Although intended primarily for students of English or literary studies, it may be of use across the arts and humanities, including Cultural Studies and History.

Acknowledgements

I would like to acknowledge the support of the students at Liverpool John Moores University, and the former Liverpool Polytechnic, who contributed much to the conception of this book over the last 15 years, and whose robust discussions and insightful writing I feel have made the introduction of literary theory a worthwhile project.

I would also like to thank colleagues who have helped to make theory and teaching a meaningful and enjoyable experience, in particular Mike Pudlo, David Amigoni, Elspeth Graham, Timothy Ashplant and Jeff Wallace. I would also like to thank Christopher Wheeler for his patience and forbearance in the preparation of this second edition, and Julia Atherton for helping with the preparation of the manuscript. Last, but not least, my gratitude is due to Glenda, Annie and Duncan who in their various ways made writing this book possible.

1 Points of departure

The place of literary theory in the study of what is still most commonly called 'English' has become increasingly important in recent years. Not so long ago – indeed when I studied for a degree in 'English Language and Literature' in the early 1970's – literary theory did not appear anywhere as a topic in the curriculum. There was an option course in the history of literary criticism, which as we shall see is a rather different area, and there was considerable attention given to the history of the English language from Anglo-Saxon and Middle English to the twentieth century, but little attention was paid to any of the issues which informed or underpinned the ways in which students read and study literature. There was little consideration of what 'English' or 'literature' consisted of, how the field of study or discipline had been established and how literary criticism functioned as a way of knowing or understanding texts. To oversimplify the activity of 'reading English' then, many students read 'works' which were written by 'authors' from certain 'periods' and these seemed fairly unproblematical or obvious categories. There were healthy debates on interpretation, usually focused around 'character', before the discussion usually closed on a particular and, one hoped at that time, definitive meaning.

For a variety of reasons teachers and students of literature have more recently come to look at these activities, categories, and the values implied by them, rather differently. Many courses which involve the study of literary texts now address questions and issues raised through literary theory which previously might have been ignored or considered as obvious or common sense and, therefore, unchallengeable ideas or concepts. Literary theory has figured increasingly on syllabuses in many institutions since the 1980s; now it is unlikely that a student of English Literature would not engage directly with aspects of literary theory and, arguably, a working knowledge of some of the fundamental areas is essential for degree or equivalent level study. This may take the form of a course in its own right: a core or option element of a degree programme.

Perhaps more significantly, though, theory is becoming evident implicitly in many courses which may be conceived around more conventional and traditional ways of organizing selections of literary texts for study such as: genre (novel, poetry or drama); period (centuries, decades or other variants); movements (e.g. Romanticism, Modernism); author(s) (selections of 'great', and sometimes not so great, writers). In the latter case the criteria for the arrangement and selection of literary texts – and also what is meant by the category of 'English' or 'literature' – can no longer be taken for granted. We might say that just as our reading experiences change as we move from childhood to adulthood, so that we read with a different awareness recognizing that narratives are invented or constructed in various ways which utilize certain devices and techniques – we cease to be 'innocent' readers – similarly, literary study has moved from a position which viewed literature as a predominantly 'natural' phenomenon to a more questioning approach which now interrogates many aspects which were previously considered unquestionable, self-evident or natural.

The advent of literary theory has been received in Britain with mixed responses. In the 1970s European literary theory, or rather theorists, became increasingly prominent: indeed it is perhaps significant that the writers of literary theory were sometimes given more prominence than their ideas – and still are in some quarters. There were heated debates in journals, newspapers and academic institutions so that there appeared to be a polarization between radical new ideas, often emphasized as foreign in origin, grouped together under the monolithic term 'theory', and more traditional views which might be characterized by terms such as humanism, common sense or tradition. Certainly groups existed which were strongly opposed to any change in English studies as constituted prior to the advent of literary theory, as there still are today. The phrase 'the crisis in English studies' was quite common by the early 1980s, and it was significant that a number of new areas of academic study arose in institutions of higher education at this time, such as Cultural Studies and Communication Studies, which were challenging in various ways both the content and the methodologies of conventional English courses as well as disrupting the monopoly which had existed on literary culture in academic circles. Such has been the impact of literary theory since the 1980s that it is virtually impossible for a literary critic to write today without an awareness of literary theory, and it would seem equally difficult for a student of literature to ignore ideas which have affected ways of reading literary texts and have become increasingly assimilated into the mainstream discourse of literary criticism.

It could be argued that there is a danger of overemphasizing literary theory, and now that the 'moment' of theory of the early to mid-1980s has passed, literary studies can return to concentrate again on more familiar matters. It has also been argued that literary theory has been an integral feature of literary study since, certainly in western cultures, there have been literary forms whether oral, performed or written and read, although perhaps not always so prominent as in recent times. Both of these views are valid, but I think that in particular the advent of twentieth-century European literary theory and its somewhat belated assimilation into English literary studies has contributed significantly to redrawing the map of what we now think of as 'English Literature' – if indeed we can still refer to such a subject with confidence. Earlier manifestations of literary theory, from Aristotle onwards, need to be acknowledged and it is important to recognize that wherever there is an established literary culture there usually are also related critical discourses. However, this introductory guide is mainly concerned with twentieth-century theories and the impact they have had on the ways in which literature is read, studied and enjoyed.

This book is intended as an introduction to some aspects of literary theory and I have tried to indicate further reading where possible for those who wish to pursue their studies in particular directions. I have also tried to link, where possible, views associated with more traditional literary criticism with those arising from literary theory which might be seen to challenge or modify them. As we shall see though, it would be erroneous to assume that literary theory offers foolproof formulas for interpretation or, on the other hand, that it is just an alternative way of reading. It would also be dangerous to view literary theory as a set of accessories or as a kind of bolt-on mechanism for studying literature. The worst approaches to literary theory are those which separate it from the activities of reading and critical interpretation; to that end I have tried, wherever possible and within the constraints of length, to offer examples of theory in practice in the following chapters to illustrate how theory and text interact. Literary theory is a complex and shifting area, unlike some previous critical orthodoxies, and characterized more by difference than consensus.

2 What is literary theory?

Literature and literary theory

In identifying an area called *literary theory,* it might be supposed that literature itself is a readily definable phenomenon. Certainly the term 'literature' is frequently used in ways which would suggest that it is not a problematic concept. Libraries for example have systems for cataloguing literary texts which mark them out clearly from other kinds of writing. Newspapers and magazines carry reviews of novels and poetry in clearly identifiable sections. Universities and Colleges still have literature courses taken by certain students, and so on. And yet, if we look at the ways in which such institutions construct the body of writing denominated by such terms as 'literature' or 'English', then we can certainly see differences emerging; such differences are often clearly observable between academia and popular institutions, but also within academia. These differences vary according to the contexts in which 'literature' is located, so that clearly we might expect to come across a different selection of books in the literature section of a newsagents on a railway station from that on the syllabus of a course in twentieth-century literature at degree level – though why this is the case is an interesting question which we shall return to later. The differences are not only cultural but also historical: literature has been defined, usually implicitly, in markedly different ways over the last hundred years. Even in what might appear to be a common context, that of academic institutions from school syllabuses to degree courses, there are very divergent conceptions of literature and conflicting ideas as to what constitutes a text worthy of study on a syllabus. Various institutions have sought to appropriate a particular kind of literature and invest it with apparently universal values and truths, and the study of literature under the title of 'English' since the late nineteenth century is a good illustration of one of the main ways in which English (rather than British) academic culture sought to homogenize and organicize the study of literature.

The English Association, founded in 1907, was the main body which sought to develop the study of an 'English' literary culture in educational institutions, promoting the concept of culture tied to moral improvement which Matthew Arnold had initiated in the nineteenth century. Arnold's view of culture as 'the best that is thought and known in the world' was to be implemented largely through the medium of literature: the study of the classics and subsequently late nineteenth- and early twentieth-century poetry. Much of this poetry indulged in pseudo-classical language and literary forms combined with pastoral myths of a rural and timeless England; Rupert Brooke's 'The Old Vicarage Granchester' (1912) is typical of the poetry which came to represent such 'Englishness'. Several critics have argued that the study of literature and the cultural institution of 'English' became substitutes for established religion, which was waning rapidly during this period. Literature was able to offer a similar kind of experience, and with the recent increases in the electoral franchise and the advent of mass literacy it was important that the state instilled appropriate civilized values in its subjects. Following the establishment of the English Association, the Government report on *The Teaching of English in England* (1921) chaired by the quintessential English poet Sir Henry Newbolt (of 'Play up! play up! and play the game' fame), consolidated the core position of English in the educational curriculum.[1]

Rather than viewing literature as a homogeneous body which is made up of works which have similar characteristics and which are read in similar ways by an undifferentiated audience, we could see it as an area which is, and has been historically, in a state of flux. As terms, 'literature' and 'literary' do not have stable and singular meanings but complex and plural ones. Further to this, 'literature', both as a body of writing and the moral and aesthetic qualities generally associated with it, can be seen as sites of struggle where meanings are contested rather than possessing timeless and universal values and truths as they have sometimes been represented as doing.

Literary theory, or rather *theories*, do offer various ways of defining literature, or at least thinking about what the issues might be in attempting any kind of definition. They are not necessarily compatible with each other, and recent commentators on the body of writing denominated as literary theory have drawn attention increasingly to the different and at times conflicting attitudes to be found between various theoretical positions. Literary theory as an area of knowledge then does not propose or offer any easy or watertight solutions as to

what literature is, or how it should be studied, but this is not necessarily a negative quality.

Two fundamental concepts relating to the study of literature arise
from literary theory which have not always been apparent in non-
theoretical approaches. First, as I have suggested in outline above,
literature becomes a problematic and heterogeneous area: we might
perhaps talk about 'Englishes' rather than 'English' in surveying the
ways in which it functions culturally and historically as a form of
writing and knowledge. Secondly, the activities associated with the
study of literature, from reading to criticism, need to be constantly
reassessed.

We might consider the discourse of literary theory as a double-
edged weapon: on the one hand it can explain or demystify some of the
assumptions or values implicit in literature and literary criticism, but
on the other hand we should not let the 'truths' which emerge from
theoretical texts stand unchallenged. Perhaps this rather cautious
approach and potentially endless activity of appraisal and reappraisal
of terms and the judgements or values they convey is one of the more
general features of literary theories: they tend towards a self-
consciousness or self-reflexivity that more traditional criticism has
eschewed and this self-consciousness is centred most often around
language – the language of the text being studied and the language
which is brought to bear on that text as it is read and interpreted.

Literary criticism and literary theory

Literary criticism has established itself as the main activity associated
with the academic study of literature, and the terms and categories
which it employs also need to be interrogated. It has been the practice
to use terms such as 'author', 'character' or 'reader' as if they were
unproblematic, as if they are quite natural and given aspects of
literature and its study. By the same token, we should not allow
categories which emerge in theoretical approaches to stand unchallenged either.

It would be helpful at this point to make a distinction between the
activities or practices of *literary criticism* and *literary theory* as these
are areas of potential confusion. Generally speaking, we can say that
literary criticism involves the reading, interpretation of and commentary on a specific text or texts which have been designated as literature.
This tends to be the predominant activity associated with literary
study: it is practised by professional critics and circulated in published
form in books and journals, and it is also practised by all students of

literature in essays, examination answers or dissertations. The rise of 'English' over the last century involved the pursuit of literary criticism as its main activity. The term 'criticism' begins to achieve a significant prominence in association with 'English' and literary studies from the late nineteenth century and continues to develop in usage in various ways in the twentieth century. The nineteenth-century poet and cultural critic Matthew Arnold began to use the term 'criticism' with particular emphasis, for example in his essay on 'The Function of Criticism at the Present Time' (1867). The term 'practical criticism' introduced by the twentieth-century literary critic I.A. Richards, and its subsequent adoption for teaching and assessment activities, are examples of how it became a central feature of English studies. Prominent 'critics', such as F.R. Leavis, became identified as the key practitioners of criticism; it is noticeable that several authors of literary works also wrote literary criticism, for example Henry James or T.S. Eliot.

Although *criticism* is a very broad umbrella term which covers various approaches to and attitudes about literature, there are two conventions or assumptions which tend to be inherent in its practice in both the activity of criticizing and critical discourse. The first is that criticism is secondary to literature itself: criticism is posterior to the literary text. The second is that critical interpretations or judgements seem to assume that the literary text which they are addressing is unquestionably literature: that literature is a natural, self-evident category and so in turn are the critical views arising from it (the implications of this will be considered in Chapter 4, under 'Ideology').

However, some of the approaches to literature and literary criticism which have developed through theoretical work would offer rather different ways of seeing things. First of all, the kinds of procedures, methods and values implicit in the assumptions above would need to be made explicit: when we say a work is 'literary' and when we analyse aspects of it in detail, and then if we were to consider it good, bad and so on, we need to understand how these activities themselves function and how such judgements are arrived at. Literary criticism, rather than being secondary to literature, can be seen as a means of constructing the body of writing and knowledge which it appears to take as its object of study; in other words, literature can be seen as a product of and dependent on criticism rather than the other way round. It is certainly the case that criticism is inevitably chronologically posterior in the discussion of the texts which it addresses, but this does not mean to say that that criticism is dependent on literature in the sense that its only function is to comment on literary texts in ways which seem to reflect their content. Rather it can be argued that both the body of writing designated as 'literature' from the late nineteenth century onwards by critics such as Matthew Arnold through to F.R. Leavis, and the identification of 'literary' qualities and characteristics such as 'tone', 'character', 'moral vision' and so on, are constructed primarily through the discourses of literary criticism and do not have their origins in the literary text as such. To put it another way, there would be no literature as we understand the term without literary criticism.

The idea that literature had its being or essential meaning independent of criticism is one which Matthew Arnold fostered in his concept of the 'disinterestedness' of the critic; criticism should 'see the object as in itself it really is', he insisted. This view of the critic as a disinterested or neutral figure, objectively examining the literary work, is one of the main features which came to be associated with literary criticism as a formal activity and which students of literature were supposed to acquire. It is somewhat at odds with the view of literature as 'experience', a subjective and individual phenomenon, where 'feeling' counts a great deal; as D.H. Lawrence asserted, 'a critic must be emotionally alive in every fibre.'[2] Literary criticism seemed to have little difficulty in assimilating such contradictory positions. Some literary theorists, however, as I have already suggested, would see 'literature', the 'literary' and the relationship of literary criticism to these areas rather differently. As we shall see in more detail later on, they saw a need to say what literature was, to identify the historical, cultural, formal and linguistic properties which can allow us to talk about the 'literary' in more specific terms. Further to this, literary theory recognizes that the assumptions which some criticism has made about writers, readers and their relationship to what we take to be 'reality', need to be questioned and reformulated and this process may alter the ways in which we read and interpret.

Perhaps here then we can make a distinction between *literary criticism* and *literary theory*. If we say that *criticism* involves the reading, analysis, explication and interpretation of texts which are designated literary, then *literary theory* should do two things. It ought to provide us with a range of criteria for identifying literature in the first place and an awareness of these criteria should inform our critical practice (some of these are examined in the discussions of theories of 'Language' in Chapter 3, and in the section on 'Ideology' in Chapter 4). It should also make us aware of the methods and procedures which we employ in the practice of literary criticism, so that we not only interrogate the text but also the ways in which we read and interpret the text. Strictly speaking, we should make a further distinction

between 'literary theory' and 'critical theory', in that liter
primarily concerned with what 'literature' and the '
whereas critical theory is concerned with the nature of cri...
critical practice. The two aspects tend to be subsumed under the
general category of 'literary theory', and indeed some theorists are
more often discussing critical theory than literary theory, which points
to the flexibility, or perhaps imprecision, of terminology which has
constantly dogged literary studies in unfortunate ways. Clearly,
though, the two areas of theory are not mutually exclusive categories,
in the same way that literary criticism and literary theory are not
totally separate: indeed they should inform each other and so have an
interdependent relationship. The diagram below suggests how we
might envisage the relationships between *literature, literary criticism*
and *literary theory:*

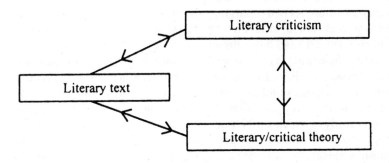

This does not represent a complete model of the literary and critical
processes: there are obvious absences, in particular the figures of the
author and the reader which are usually thought of as fundamental to
studying literature. Perhaps though at this point we might note that
some theoretical approaches are not so concerned with traditional
conceptions of the figure of the author, and would not take the author
as the axiomatic point of departure in thinking about literature in the
sense of either a body of writing or an individual text.

Literature and experience

One of the most difficult issues in relating reading and interpretation
to theoretical arguments is that our understanding of a poem, novel or
play is inevitably determined by our *experience* of it, and this will be
further determined by our previous experiences, both literary and
non-literary. But experience, though, can mean very different things,

and as a term is capable of containing quite contradictory ideas: for example, in common sense terms the experience of language is that the world or 'reality' is one thing and language another and we can use language to reflect the world. Yet theories of language would indicate that this assumed relationship is more complex and rather different and can challenge our common sense experience (this is dealt with more extensively in Chapter 3 under 'Language').

The study of literature has been strongly associated with the realm of experience and related terms like 'feeling' and 'emotion'. As such, literary study has tended to be placed in opposition to the sciences and the social sciences by perceptions of academic subjects, especially in British institutions. Theory was recognized as having a place in the study of subjects such as Physics or Chemistry and could also be seen explicitly in Sociology or Philosophy. When it comes to subjects which are usually considered as belonging to the arts or humanities though, theory is often seen as marginal or even irrelevant. The study of History does not always involve the study of historical theory in explicit form, and as I have already suggested, the study of English or literature in Britain has been very resistant to theoretical arguments and approaches. F.R. Leavis saw literary criticism as quite distinct from the disciplines and methods of Sociology or Philosophy; he felt that the 'trained frequentation of literature alone' was at the centre of literary study in which a full understanding of 'concrete human experience' could be gained.[3] In particular, the concepts of feeling and emotion constituted the core of the experiential axis of literary study, often under the heading of 'practical criticism', where the reader was supposedly able to identify with the experience contained within the literary text or with that of the writer transmitted through the text. But exactly whose feelings and emotions is a question which was usually not addressed; literature seems to have offered a form of transcendent, universal experience which literary criticism could identify – almost intuitively in some cases.

This region of experience qualified by feeling however has become increasingly problematic as theoretical enquiry has generated views questioning the nature and primacy of experience as a form of understanding and knowledge. The central issue which a number of theoretical arguments have exposed is: whose experience are we talking about in this kind of criticism? Experience is subjective, relative, individually and historically variable; in the case of literature it is generated by language, which is a further complication, although perhaps many critics of the experiential school would either ignore the language or see it as merely a secondary aspect of, or medium for, experience. The multiple and problematic aspects of experience tended to be suppressed in much critical practice. Rather than revealing the plural, variable nature of interpretation, stressing the importance of the context of the reader in terms of history, gender and class, and his/her consequent relationship to the literary text, such criticism often aimed at establishing a general or universal truth common to all people which was apparently validated by individually shared experience. The individual experience articulated more often than not placed little emphasis on differences between readers; indeed the language of much critical writing has assumed that all readers are by definition male and usually implied a shared set of cultural values and interpretive framework.

Experience as a critical touchstone, then, needs to be examined carefully. It can obscure the processes by which forms of meaning arise and can lead to the acceptance of values or 'truths' which are part of a much larger cultural context than that of the work in question. On the other hand, experience and theory need not be opposed to each other: rather than invalidating the experience of reading, theory can enhance and liberate it. As we shall see, by challenging some of the dominant conventions and assumptions within traditional modes of criticism, literary theory can lead to a much fuller and more profound understanding of literary texts and the forms of experience generated by them.

Literary tradition

Related to experience, the idea of tradition has been very significant in the process of constructing the subject area or discipline of English and to the practice of criticism. If 'criticism' became one of the keywords for approaches to literature in the later nineteenth century in association with concepts of culture, morality and civilization, then one of the keywords in the earlier twentieth century is 'tradition' which gave literature and literary criticism a particular inflection and set of values. A short but very influential essay by T.S. Eliot entitled 'Tradition and the Individual Talent' (1919) argued that literature embodies timeless qualities and values which can be seen as a form of cultural heritage:

> the historical sense involves a perception, not only of the pastness of the past, but of its presence; the historical sense compels a man to write not merely with his own generation in his bones, but with a feeling that the

whole of the literature of Europe from Homer and within it the whole of the literature of his whole country has a simultaneous existence and composes a simultaneous order. This historical sense, which is the sense of the timeless and the temporal together, is what makes a writer traditional.[4]

The sense of a single, unified 'tradition' became central to the way in which literature came to be viewed. At the time when he was writing *The Waste Land* (1922), on surface appearances a very fragmented, experimental literary text, Eliot was also suggesting that literature and its study consisted primarily of a sense of unity and value which transcended any specific historical moment. In fact, the argument de-historicizes literature both from the past and the present in any material sense and instead promotes a notion of a kind of spiritual history which is dependent on the intuitive recognition of shared human experience, similar to F.R. Leavis's view of the role of literary criticism. This is further bolstered by two more theses: that literature is an impersonal activity in which the individual writer's or reader's experience is subordinated to and informed by the larger sense of experience as tradition, and that there is, at least from the mid-seventeenth century onwards, a division between experience and language.

Rather than arguing along reasoned theoretical lines, Eliot can be seen as representative of what could be called the metaphysical approach to literature. By 'metaphysical', I mean that he assumes unquestionably that literature – or a certain kind of literature – is a repository of absolute value and truth which does not need to be demonstrated and cannot be challenged. 'Experience' and 'tradition' are never rigorously defined, even though 'rigour' supposedly characterized the activity of 'practical criticism', the kind of close reading of literary works which was much favoured from the 1920s onwards.

Practical criticism was initially a way of reading developed by one of Eliot's followers, I.A. Richards. Richards did attempt to put literary criticism on to some kind of rational or scientific footing by suggesting a reading method: it is significant that Richards, and another major early critic, William Empson, came to literature from scientific aca-demic backgrounds and in some respects this is evident in their attempts to shift criticism to a more analytical plane. However, the main critical categories which Richards advocates in his book *Practical Criticism: A Study of Literary Judgement* (1929), 'sense', 'tone', 'feel-ing' and 'intention' seem highly unscientific, especially in the light of more recent critical and literary theory. F.R. Leavis similarly advo-cated a reading method called 'close reading' which seemed a central principle of critical practice as he envisaged it. And yet if we look at the kinds of judgements and conclusions which Eliot and Leavis came to, they rarely seem to be the products of such rigorous close textual analysis. One would assume that such methods would pay very close attention to language and textual structures, but more often their judgements tended to be informed by ideas and values which lay outside the text and were related to the generalized areas of experience and tradition. Criticizing *The Waste Land* in his work *New Bearings in English Poetry* (1932), Leavis asserted that it revealed 'a mind fully alive in the age', but his reading is one which emphasizes the poem's sense of the loss and fragmentation of an earlier literary and cultural heritage. Anything contemporary is treated derogatively in the poem and largely ignored by Leavis. When Leavis talks about being fully alive to language or 'the concrete of human experience', it is as though his metaphors are attempting to solidify an essentially non-materialist critical approach which does not engage with the text either as language or history.

Eliot, Leavis and others assembled a collection of literary works which came to form what has become known as the 'canon', that is, a body of works selected and elevated to canonical status which formed the backbone of literary culture or tradition. Quite what the criteria for canonization were, was never made clear, but certainly this collection of works has formed the core of English studies since the early twentieth century. There have been over the years fine points of debate as to whether certain authors could be allowed such status. Leavis in *The Great Tradition* (1948), initially saw Dickens as lacking the perfection necessary for true greatness except for *Hard Times* (1854), which exhibited 'distinctive creative genius ... controlled throughout to a unifying and organizing significance', but he later relented and placed him in the literary pantheon alongside the unquestionable greats as he saw them of Jane Austen and George Eliot. What is clear though is that authors or works so elected were designated thus by rather vague qualities which go back to T.S. Eliot and Matthew Arnold; and whilst debates went on as to the relative greatness of Milton or Shelley, vast areas of writing were ignored. Popular literature was not considered in any way literary, indeed it was perceived as a threat to great literature and the moral values associated with it. Leavis saw popular literature as a form of cultural pollution and argued for the value of high culture in a pamphlet published in 1930 called 'Mass Civilization and Minority Culture'; the same kinds of views underpinned the journal *Scrutiny* which Leavis founded in 1932 and edited until its demise in 1953.

To conclude, the critical position represented by Leavis and going back to Matthew Arnold is untheorized, at least in the recent sense of literary theory. Indeed the idea that criticism could be in any way theoretical was anathema to Leavis, as he made clear in an essay called 'Literary Criticism and Philosophy' in his book *The Common Pursuit* (1952). In this essay, Leavis argues that literary criticism has nothing in common with philosophy and that any 'theoretical system' would be alien to it. His definitions of the critic and the practice of literary criticism use the kind of vocabulary which is indicative of the 'life/ experience' view of literature:

> By the critic of poetry I understand the complete reader: the ideal critic is the ideal reader. The reading demanded by poetry is of a quite different kind from that demanded by philosophy. . . . Words in poetry invite us, not to 'think about' and judge but to 'feel into' or 'become' . . . The critic's aim is, first, to realize as sensitively and completely as possible this or that which claims his attention . . . As he matures in experience of the new thing he asks, explicitly and implicitly: 'Where does this come? How does it stand in relation to . . . ? How relatively important does it seem?' And the organization into which it settles as a constituent in becoming 'placed' is an organization of similarly 'placed' things, things that have found their bearings with regard to one another, and not a theoretical system or a system determined by abstract considerations.[5]

Leavis could be seen here as attempting to formulate some kind of critical method approximating to what we would now think of as a theoretical position even though he seems to be resisting such an approach. On the other hand his language, and argument in so far as there is one, are extremely vague and abstract: ironically, exactly what Leavis appears to complain against in theory and philosophy. Literary theorists such as Terry Eagleton[6] have questioned Leavis's views, arguing that he does not make explicit the processes by which he evaluates a literary text, and further that the kind of criticism he practised can lead to mystification: that is, rather than clarifying and making explicit the ways in which judgements are reached and literary texts 'placed' in a certain order, they are actually obscured. The effect of this is to make 'natural' by concealment or disguise the cultural and historical implications of such criticism. The kind of 'experience' Leavis is invoking here seems undefined, and remote from rather than part of most readers' experiences; presumably it is the product of reading particular literary works combined with a special sensibility which allows us intuitively to recognize such works and evaluate them.

By arguing on the one hand that 'feeling', 'life' and 'experience' are central to literary criticism Leavis and his predecessors would seem to be bringing literature much closer to the reader than some theoretical approaches might appear to; there is something apparently accessible and commonsensical about such empirical language. However, such language obscures the very areas it seeks to identify and clarify: 'feeling', 'life' and 'experience' are used in very general, abstract ways which ignore the specificity of literary production and consumption and imply that there is one timeless, unified, universal way of reading which we all may ultimately achieve, or at least glimpse, which in turn exemplifies the larger body of canonical literature as tradition. Such criticism only allows readers to recognize certain ideas and values whilst excluding or marginalizing others.

The question of 'recognition', of how we come to understand or know certain things as good, bad, true or false, is a very important area; this will be examined in Chapter 4 under 'Ideology'. Leavis's notion of 'placing' texts will also be developed in Chapter 5, under 'Textual relations', where the ways in which interpretation and meaning arise and function will be addressed. For the rest of this chapter I want to turn to some of the assumptions and conventions central to literature and literary criticism and to see how literary theory offers perspectives on these. In some cases, as with the concept of the 'author', these may seem radical or provocative, but if they challenge our common sense views this need not be necessarily a bad thing in that it should help us to make our own positions clearer to ourselves and those with whom we discuss or communicate ideas about literature. In 1957, in a book which attempted to define the nature and function of literary criticism called *Anatomy of Criticism*, Northrop Frye lamented the lack of any systematic theory of literature; without it he felt that no text of basic principles could be written. Criticism was 'a mystery religion without a gospel', he stated. Whilst I would not want to suggest that literary theory is the gospel that Frye thought was lacking – and few theorists would want to make such a claim – there are now ideas in circulation which help to clarify what literature and literary criticism involve. And perhaps one of the things that literary theory tells us is that the gospels are themselves texts subject to interpretation: knowledge and truth are historically relative – something that the institutions of literature and literary criticism have not always acknowledged, perhaps because it is against their interests to do so.

Literary production and consumption

I have chosen to focus the rest of this chapter around two concepts employing categories which I used earlier: 'production' and 'consumption'. These terms recognize initially that literature is not timeless or in some ahistorical vacuum but subject to two contexts: that in which it is written, produced or created, and that in which it is subsequently circulated, read and consumed. Although this might appear to be an obvious distinction, the differences between these two contexts are often blurred, so that when a poem or novel is read or interpreted, confusion can arise as to whether we find meanings which are specific to a particular set of reading relations which form the reading context, or are finding meanings which we assume were there initially and remain constant. This division can be further complicated once we recognize that a literary text's meanings change over time; so that we could argue that *Hamlet* (1603) has come to mean something very different for an audience in the 1990s than for an audience in the first years of the seventeenth century. We need to be aware that our views about what it might have meant then are themselves an act of interpretation or reconstruction and the idea of establishing some kind of 'original' meaning is very problematic and questionable.

The division between production and consumption is helpful in thinking about changing attitudes towards the reading and handling of literature in literary criticism and theory. This can be illustrated in simplified form thus:

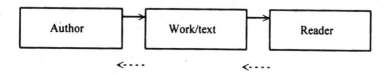

This diagram represents a common sense and therefore seemingly obvious attitude to literature which is that authors produce works which are then read by readers; the production and transmission process is assumed to be from the author to the reader and the ideas or meanings communicated would seem to originate in the author's mind which are then relayed through the poem, novel or play to the reader. The reader is then able to go back along this axis to discover the author's intention and re-experience the author's experience. The starting and usual focal point of this reading model is the author, who represents the origin and source of meanings attributed to a literary work which are viewed in the forms of intention and experience.

The diagram can also be used to illustrate in simplified form the changes in emphasis which have arisen over the last 50 years in critical approaches, more latterly informed by developments in literary and critical theory. Most criticism prior to the 1950s, and indeed much subsequently, could be described as 'author-centred': that is focusing on the author along the lines of the common sense model outlined above. However, a number of critics began to question this assumption in the 1940s and 1950s, arguing that attention should be focused primarily on the literary work or text and not on the author. They suggested that the critic's main concern was with the language and form of the text being read and not with the author who produced it. Indeed, developments arising from this approach argue that meaning is produced not by the author but through the language of the text. More recently, a number of theorists who have introduced a particular area of literary theory usually known as 'reader theory' or 'reception theory', have focused not on the author or the text but on the reader as the central figure in the reading and critical process.

The author and authority

The concept of the author has been central to literary criticism and the discipline of English Literature since the late nineteenth century, when they became recognized as fields of knowledge. Criticism and biography became at times virtually indistinguishable from one another, so that the more you knew about an author's life, the more you were likely to understand the literature he/she wrote. Literature was not seen as separable from the figure who produced it; approaches to Shakespeare are indicative of this. For example, A.C. Bradley lectured on 'Shakespeare the Man' (1904) and attempted to construct a portrait of Shakespeare's sensibility from a reading of his plays. Although he admits that our biographical knowledge of Shakespeare is small', this does not inhibit his conjecturing on intimate aspects of Shakespeare's mind and feelings and wanting to understand 'the character and the attitude towards life, of the human being who seems to us to have understood best our common human nature.'[7] Thirty-five years later, we find a similar approach in Peter Alexander's *Shakespeare's Life and Art* (1939) which locates the plays in a bio-graphical scheme that underpins the critical argument, beginning with a portrait of Shakespeare's upbringing and education. F.R. Leavis, writing more recently on the irony of Swift, recognizes the distinction between biography and literary criticism but simultaneously proceeds to weld them together again:

I wish to discuss Swift's writings – to examine what they are; and they are (as the extant commentary bears witness) of such a kind that it is peculiarly difficult to discuss them without shifting the focus of discussion to the kind of man that Swift was . . . In the attempt to say what makes these writings so remarkable, reference to the man who wrote them is indeed necessary.[8]

Whilst some debate had taken place on the relationship between author and work in the late 1940s and early 1950s, in particular over the issue of intentionality as we shall see shortly, more radical shifts have occurred since the 1960s. These have challenged traditional assumptions regarding the author as the originator or producer of the literary work and questioned the author's authority over the text. The best example of this argument is Roland Barthes' essay 'The Death of the Author', published in 1968. In this essay, what we might call the 'biographical fallacy' is attacked:

The image of literature to be found in ordinary culture is tyrannically centred on the author, his person, his life, his tastes, his passions, while criticism still consists for the most part in saying that Baudelaire's work is the failure of Baudelaire the man, Van Gogh's his madness, Tchaikovsky's his vice. The explanation of a work is always sought in the man or woman who produced it, as if it were always in the end, through the more or less transparent allegory of fiction, the voice of a single person, the author 'confiding' in us.[9]

Barthes argues that 'it is language which speaks not the author', and that we need to abandon an author-centred approach if we are to realize the full range of meanings contained within a literary text. Once a text is in circulation the umbilical cord, so to speak, between author and text is cut and the text leads an independent existence. Barthes also raises questions which we shall examine shortly about the individuality of the author in the writing process. He concludes by arguing that the 'multiplicity' of meanings which make up a text is focused not on the author, but on the reader: 'a text's unity lies not in its origin but in its destination', and that we need to overthrow the myth of the author: 'the birth of the reader must be at the cost of the death of the Author.' Barthes' use of 'myth' is closely allied to ideology in the sense that the traditional view of the author is one which obscures and controls the potential meanings in a literary text – the myth of the author operates as a form of cultural control. We should not forget though that Barthes' essay is itself a text produced at a particular historical moment, and 1968 was a time when there were many challenges to established authority in cultural and educational spheres; abandoning the author has a particular significance in this context as do earlier views which locate the author as the focal point of literary production. Barthes' point about the tyranny of the author could be demonstrated with the example of my own preceding discussion: many critics and theorists who consciously avoid talking about an author's position or views in relation to a literary text in the light of these ideas have no such concern, it would seem, about talking of literary critics or theorists as authors – such as F.R. Leavis or Roland Barthes. (On 'text' as applicable to any form of writing – literary or non-literary – see Chapter 5, 'Textual relations'.) It is very difficult to avoid the conventions of an established discourse because it means resisting the very language which informs us about certain kinds of knowledge, and of course inevitably people still refer to authors when talking about literature. The important point is to be aware of the significance of the 'author' when handling the term even if we cannot – or do not wish to – abandon it.

A more historical approach to authorship is taken by Michel Foucault in an essay called 'What is an Author?' (1969).[10] In his discussion the figure of the author is linked to the emergence in western culture of what Foucault calls 'individualization', that is the central place occupied by named individuals in the way that forms of knowledge are organized. The author thus confers identity and status on various kinds of writing as they circulate in society; he or she provides a point of recognition, 'a solid and fundamental unit'. Foucault calls the ways in which an author's name is used to control the circulation of literature the 'author-function' and suggests that it is actually a way of restricting the forms of reading and the meanings which can arise from a text – a similar view to that of Roland Barthes above. His argument is that the figure of the author was not so important to literary works before the seventeenth or eighteenth centuries, when the individual author's seal of approval was not needed to validate the 'truth' or authority and works were accepted anonymously. With emergence of bourgeois society and the new emphasis on ownership and property laws, combined with the growth in scientific knowledge as a way of explaining the world, literary texts became more significant as products and indicators of individualism, and occupied a rather different terrain.

Foucault's view of the author-function is that it serves an ideological purpose: that is, authors are commonly represented as being the source of creative talent, genius and imagination but function in an opposite way to this. The labelling of works according to authors can be viewed as an impediment to the free circulation of knowledge in that the works are already 'placed' in a particular system of knowledge and value governed by conceptions and conventions of authorship and biography. What seems to be for Leavis a question of judgement, experience and intuition in knowing or 'placing' a literary work becomes for Foucault a largely predetermined and ideological process which functions to maintain knowledge and consequently power in specific and dominant sections of society. The author-function is thus a containment strategy which positions literature and the reader in relation to each other and does not permit the freedom of response which is commonly ascribed to it through phrases like 'the author's imagination'. One final point which Foucault makes is that the convention of the author does not precede a literary text, but rather follows it; this is an inversion of one aspect of the process of literary production as it is normally conceived. What he means by this is that the idea we have of 'Shakespeare' or 'Wordsworth' arises after works by such authors have been in public circulation; and part of the organizing and validating of literary works in our culture is achieved by constructing the persona of the author retrospectively in relation to his or her work. The emergence in the late nineteenth century of a series of biographies of 'great' writers, for example *The English Men of Letters* series including *Samuel Johnson* (1878), *Alexander Pope* (1880), *Jonathan Swift* (1882), *George Eliot* (1902), and *The Dictionary of National Biography*, both edited by Leslie Stephen, are good examples which arise in parallel with 'English' as a subject and the development of the discourse of literary criticism.[11]

It may well be that the arguments of Barthes and Foucault seem extreme and unacceptable, and I would not want to suggest that they are definitive accounts of the figure of the author. As Barthes and Foucault themselves would acknowledge, the figure of the author constitutes a site for debate and has been invested with various significances historically; this must apply to their own arguments too. However, their ideas are provocative and do lead us to question what have been taken as axiomatic 'truths' regarding literature. The essays in question seek to theorize and problematize the 'author' so that it is no longer an assumed or 'natural' category.

We shall be returning to ways of understanding the author in Chapter 5, 'Textual relations'.

Intention and meaning

Along with the traditional view of the primacy of the author in literary production, it was usually thought that an author's intention was central to any act of interpretation on the part of the reader. The question of *intention* can be seen as one of the issues around which literary or critical theory began to challenge such assumptions, at least in American and British circles.

When I.A. Richards formulated his critical categories in *Practical Criticism* in an attempt to organize the reading of poetry, although it seemed that the reader's attention should be focused mainly on the text under scrutiny, the approach was still centred ultimately on the author's intention. The idea of knowing or establishing an author's intention, and that this explains a literary work, has become increasingly problematic. Most authors do not provide statements of intention; indeed some contemporary writers such as Samuel Beckett or Harold Pinter have deliberately avoided making statements about their works when interviewed, as if they had no more right than anyone else to comment on them, seeming to deny any responsibility for them once they are in public circulation. Even where we do have an apparently clear statement of intention, there are problems in reading or positioning a work definitively in relation to an author. At what point does such a statement arise: before a work is written, during its composition, or retrospectively? W.H. Auden's intentions regarding his poem 'Spain' (c.1937) clearly changed in that he chose to omit it from collections of his work in later life. In a post-Freudian era where notions about the importance and even determining role of the unconscious aspect of our minds have been accepted – especially in relation to the creative or imaginative side of our thinking – how can we be sure that an author's professed intention is the real or only intention? Even if we can establish an intention, or criteria for what might constitute an intention, how reliable will these be? One way of looking at 'intention' as a category is that it seems to simplify the critical process in fixing a work on a definitive, uncontested point or source. It is an essentialist approach, implying that there is ultimately a right, correct underlying meaning which is eventually accessible to everyone. This is a convenient way of organizing knowledge, and equally a way of ensuring that certain ideas and, more significantly, ways of understanding those ideas endure.

In America in the late 1940s and early 1950s a school of literary criticism arose which became known as the 'New Criticism', composed of the self-styled 'New Critics'. Their approach to literature was *formalist*, and sometimes called *structuralist*, but not to be confused with the subsequent movement which arose mainly in France in the 1960s also known as *Structuralism*, though the two have some areas in common. As the term suggests, *formalism* is a critical approach which is more concerned with the literary artefact and its form rather than with the artist or historical context: increasingly the meaning of a work was seen to reside in the text rather than in the author's mind. The 'experience' was not so much that which the author originally had and then communicated through language to a reader, but rather it was located in the literary work itself. In order to shift the emphasis from author to work, the main principle of this critical approach was based around a concept called 'the intentional fallacy', arguing that an author's intention (assuming it could be established) was not necessarily a guide to a work's meaning; 'The Intentional Fallacy' (1946) is the title of the essay by two of the New Critics, W.K. Wimsatt and M.C. Beardsley, in which this argument is established. One of the most helpful definitions of the concept is in René Wellek's and Austin Warren's book *Theory of Literature* (1949):

> The whole idea that the 'intention' of the author is the proper subject of literary history seems, however, quite mistaken. The meaning of a work of art is not exhausted by, or even equivalent to, its intention. As a system of values it leads an independent life.[12]

In displacing the author and intentionality, this kind of approach constructed a new centre on which to focus the reader's attention: not the author but the work or text. This was a very significant shift in that it anticipated Barthes' 'death of the author' in allowing meaning to be located in the work rather than in the author's mind. It broke, or seemed to break, with what has also been called the 'humanist fallacy', which Terry Eagleton explains:

> Such a view of literature always tends to find its distinguishing characteristic – the fact that it is written – somehow disturbing: the print, in all its cold impersonality, interposes its ungainly bulk between ourselves and the author. If only we could talk to Cervantes directly! Such an attitude 'dematerializes' literature, strives to reduce its material density as language to the intimate spiritual encounter of living 'persons'. It goes along with the liberal humanist suspicion of all that cannot be immediately reduced to the interpersonal, from feminism to factory production. It is not, in the end, concerned with regarding the literary text as a text at all.[13]

This shift might be seen as a kind of critical Copernican revolution in that meaning now orbited around the text and not the author. Wellek and Warren go on to suggest that, 'The total meaning of a work of art cannot be defined merely in terms of its meaning for the author and his contemporaries. It is rather the result of a process of accretion, i.e. the history of its criticism by many readers in many ages.' The idea that a literary text is a kind of palimpsest, a surface on which the text is in effect rewritten as it is processed through its reading and critical history, is one which will be examined in more detail in Chapter 5 under 'Textual relations'. However, this revised critical model also has problems and there have been further developments away from it as we shall see.

One problem was that the work or text itself became overemphasized: the organic unity of experience shifted from the author's imagination to the aesthetics of literary form and there was still the sense of an essential meaning to be discovered which had to be unlocked from the text. The text became reified, an object and end in itself rather than merely a transparent window on to the author. The titles of critical books which follow this approach are revealing: *The Verbal Icon* (1954), *The Well-Wrought Urn* (1947) or *Experience into Words* (1963), suggesting that the words are still really secondary to the experience or meaning contained in the poem – language and meaning are still conceived as separate areas. There is too a suggestion that the author is still immanent in spite of all this, brought in by the back door, so to speak. This formalist critical model does still imply that meaning, or intention as embodied and realized in a literary work, is at the heart of the interpretive process and that it is possible to misread a work. The idea of misreading is itself highly problematic: how do we establish a 'correct' or definitive reading? The way the New Critics did it was to introduce another 'fallacy' argument which propped up their position at the other end of the author-text-reader axis, and which prevented free or plural interpretation. This was called the 'affective fallacy' through which it was argued that subjective, impressionistic responses to a poem were not adequate and ran the risk of being distortions of the organized meaning that lay in the structure of the literary text. The context for the meaning is then the text itself: its internal relations of language and form. This critical model has been attacked on two grounds. First, it suggests that meaning is transcendent and universal: it is an ahistorical view of literature which does not take into account the specific conditions of production and consumption. The emphasis on the text is aesthetic rather than material, and aesthetics can be very difficult to pin down historically as many of the ideas associated with them are to do with claims about the timelessness of truth and beauty. Second, the concept of organization implies an organizing force. Who or what is the organizer? Literary texts certainly do not arise from an impersonal vacuum. For the New Critics, this was a dilemma. In denying the author's intention and emphasizing the text, who controlled the reader's responses? The problem was negotiated by ideas such as the 'social relations' of a text, whereby the reader would be able to tune into what the author meant even if the author's intention wasn't clear or relevant, so that what mattered was the way in which the work of art at its moment of completion could be apprehended as such by a subsequent reader. This is a very idealist view of literature, implying that a perfect text can be discovered and along with it a perfect meaning; it ignores the fact that works of art change their meanings in various ways, in particular in different historical contexts. The New Critics seemed to want a critical model which had it both ways in that in abandoning the author – or at least intention – as the source of authority, the essential meaning contained in the text, like a kernel of truth, was still the true object of study.

One way in which the increasingly problematic status of the author has been negotiated was with the construction of what Wayne C. Booth called in *The Rhetoric of Fiction* (1961) the 'implied author'. The term indicates the way the sense of an author normally inheres in a text, even if the image of the author is quite distinct from what we know about the historical figure of the author. In John Fowles' novel, *The French Lieutenant's Woman* (1969), the figure of the implied author is strongly present – indeed it becomes a foregrounded fictional device – but it would be erroneous to assume that this textual effect is equivalent to the real life John Fowles who leads an independent existence from the novel. The cases of novels like Emily Brontë's *Wuthering Heights* (1847) or Ford Maddox Ford's *The Good Soldier* (1915) are more difficult in one sense because their narrative techniques obscure any impression of the author, but on the other hand they raise interesting questions about authorial control and authority. Thomas Hardy's novels are quite the opposite; it is easy to identify the third person omniscient narrator as the implied author in the text, but we should not slip into the trap of equating this figure with the historical writer. Hardy's narrators in fact do not always exhibit consistency, and we need to be careful not to let them coalesce into an undifferentiated figure either in the text or from Hardy the author.

'Work' and 'text'

So far I have referred to the individual products of literature as 'works' or 'texts' as if the two words were synonymous. Although ostensibly they appear to refer to the same object, they have acquired rather different significances and these are indicative of the differences between an approach to literature which is informed by literary theory and those involving more traditional views. Certainly the term 'text' has been used, prior to the advent of what we think of as literary theory, to signify a poem, play or novel – often to draw attention to the linguistic features of literature which can be ignored in considering questions regarding experience or intention. 'Work' on the other hand does imply more of a connection between the artefact or product and the artist or writer; it also has connotations of things being crafted and well finished. It was these kinds of distinctions which led Roland Barthes and other theorists to take a clearly defined position in relation to literary artefacts by insisting on the use of the term 'text', giving it specific meanings. Barthes makes this position clear in two essays, 'The Death of the Author' which has already been discussed, and 'From Work to Text' (1971). For him, 'work' has the sense of an artefact over which the author has total control and which reinforces the traditional model of intentionality and an author-centred approach to interpretation. It also implies notions of the author as an individual genius, a fountain of imagination and creativity producing original writing – according to Barthes a very romanticized view of literary production. His conception of the text and 'textuality' is quite a departure from this traditional view.

Ideas of 'textuality' are complex and will be examined in more detail later on, but the main ideas which Barthes and other theorists invest in 'text' as opposed to 'work' need to be introduced. First, as with some previous arguments, the author is not seen as the main producer of the text, nor is he/she necessarily to be identified with it. As Barthes puts it, 'He becomes, as it were, a paper-author: his life is no longer the origin of his fictions but a fiction contributing to his work ... the I which writes the text, it too, is never more than a paper-I.'[14] Barthes inverts the conventional view of the author controlling and producing the language of the text; for him the author too is a textual product or effect: 'it is language which speaks, not the author'. In other words, the idea of the author becomes one strand, one narrative among many, of which a text is composed. This leads on to the second point, which is that literary texts are networks of meaning, composed of various discourses: they are multi-layered in their composition. This multiplicity cannot be reduced or distilled into a single, neat, fixed meaning. A particular reading of a text may seize on one aspect and privilege it as a central meaning, but for Barthes if there is anything essential about the idea of a text, it is its plural nature: it is 'irreducible' and open to repeated readings and reinterpretation. The idea of trying to find the ultimate meaning of *Hamlet* or 'Ode to a Nightingale' (1819) would not only be futile, but would ignore the range of meanings contained in such texts. Ironically and demonstrably, previous criticism makes this point: the practice of critics successively claiming to have found the definitive interpretation of a play, poem or novel is clearly self-defeating. Thirdly, Barthes sees meaning as generated by language, or by the 'sign', as language theorists and structuralists would put it. It is language and not experience which generates meaning. The potential for a literary text generating a multiplicity of meanings is realized through the linguistic permutations available in the text and subject to the reading context: that is history and the individual reader. To suggest that a text has a particular meaning, either originating in the author's mind or from an ideal aesthetic harmonization of the text, forecloses other possibilities for reading and privileges certain critical approaches and interpretations. For Barthes and other theorists, reading and interpretation are contentious and relative activities rather than processes for establishing conformity; herein lies his conception of a healthy literary criticism and the highest form of reading pleasure constructed around a recognition of different reading positions and the play of the sign in a text. The term *play* suggests that language is not authoritatively fixed and singular, but open to a range of meanings which are fluid and can change. Barthes shifts the emphasis not only from 'work' to 'text', but also as we have seen to the reader, in a crucial statement:

> Thus is revealed the total existence of writing: a text is made up of multiple writings, drawn from many cultures into mutual relations of dialogue, parody, contestation, but there is one place where this multiplicity is focused and that place is the reader, not, as was hitherto said, the author.

Finally, Barthes and others, especially in theories associated with Cultural Studies, would use 'text' in its widest sense. That is not only high literary culture, or perhaps the canonical 'works' of 'English' Literature, but films, advertisements, paintings, and certainly popular literature as well. This breaks with traditional discipline-based conceptions of what constitutes a work or text and also places the text in a broader arena where we can begin to ask questions about whether there is something intrinsically different between so-called high and popular texts, and to examine why historically and culturally such divisions and hierarchies have arisen. In the fields of literary criticism and theory, the kinds of approaches derived from linguistics and language theory, from Cultural Studies and associated areas, have offered different perspectives and provided alternative ways of reading to what might be described as the 'great minds and great works' view.

The reader

As we can see from the preceding section, the reader is given a new role and status according to Barthes' model of literary production. Perhaps one reason why little explicit emphasis was given to the reader and the dynamics of reading is that readers have often been thought of as the least significant element in the author-text-reader axis: the role of the reader was seen as largely unproblematic and therefore not requiring any examination or explanation. Unlike the attention given to authors and works or texts, readers were thought of as passive receivers of meaning, their role assumed and naturalized in ways which did not explore the problematics of reading. An author-centred criticism, as we have seen, assumes that the author is both the origin and object of literature and interpretation respectively. A work/ text-centred criticism – such as the New Criticism of the 1940s and 1950s – with the 'poem itself' as the origin of meaning and object of criticism equally banishes the reader to a marginal or excluded position. In fact, New Criticism also developed the 'affective fallacy' (W.K. Wimsatt and M.C. Beardsley, 'The Affective Fallacy', 1949), according to which: 'It begins by trying to derive the standard of criticism from the psychological effects of the poem and ends in impressionism and relativism. The outcome ... is that the poem itself, as an object of specifically critical judgement, tends to disappear'. In effect, this removed the reader along with the author for a supposed objective criticism which concentrated on the text itself. It should be added though that not all literary texts themselves, and perhaps not all authors, recognize readers as passive and identical: Laurence Sterne's novel *Tristram Shandy* (1760–7) makes very strong demands on the reader with its direct addresses and questions which preclude any passivity. Although over 200 years later, Italo Calvino's novel *If on a winter's night a traveller* (1979, trans. 1981) accentuates the reader's role to the extent of recognizing the physical reading process:

> You are about to begin reading Italo Calvino's new novel, *If on a winter's night a traveller*. Relax. Concentrate. Dispel every other thought. Let the world around you fade. Best to close the door; the TV is always on in the next room ... Find the most comfortable position: seated, stretched out, curled up, or lying flat. Flat on your back, on your side, on your stomach. In an easy chair, on the sofa, in the rocker, the deck chair, on the hassock. In the hammock, if you have a hammock. On top of your bed, of course, or in

the bed. You can even stand on your hands, head down, in the yoga position. With the book upside down, naturally.[15]

Calvino's novel involves the reader quite explicitly in ways which more traditional realist novels, such as Hardy's *Tess of the d'Urbervilles* (1891) or Charles Dickens' *Hard Times* rarely do; this is a characteristic of much modernist and more especially postmodernist writing where the constructed nature of fiction and its relationship to the reader is recognized (see Chapter 5, under 'Postmodernism'). The physical contortions of the implied reader in *If on a winter's night a traveller* also parallel, and perhaps parody, the various interpretive reading positions which critical theory has identified.

One way in which the early literary criticism associated with the rise of 'English' established its authority was to assume that either all readers were ultimately the same or that they would achieve conformity. The fact that readers are extremely varied in terms of class, gender, history, race and culture did not seem to be significant factors in literary criticism until fairly recently. F.R. Leavis's definition of the ideal reader is typically vague: 'By the critic of poetry I understand the complete reader: the ideal critic is the ideal reader.' This is as far as Leavis is able, or wants, to go; presumably he means someone 'fully alive' to all the possibilities of meaning in a text as he puts it: this implies the inadequacy of most readers and the need to arrive at an apparently informed consensus rather than permitting more plural possibilities of reading and interpretation.

As well as the 'implied author', following Wayne C. Booth the theorist Wolfgang Iser developed the idea of the 'implied reader' (*The Implied Reader: Patterns of Communication in Prose Fiction from Bunyan to Beckett*, 1974) to help to describe the pattern of interaction between text and reader. The implied reader is distinct from the real or empirical reader; it is part of the 'structure of the text' and may be thought of more as an inscribed reader who represents a point of coherence where the various meanings and codes of a text may be understood. Following Iser, the categories of reader have multiplied quite considerably. Umberto Eco, whose novel *The Name of the Rose* (1980, trans. 1983) explores, among other fictional conventions, the reader's position, produced the concept of the 'model reader' (*The Role of the Reader: Explorations in the Semiotics of Texts*, 1981). Eco's model reader is not dissimilar to Iser's implied reader – it is a 'possible reader ... able to deal interpretively with the expressions in the same way that the author deals generatively with them', a set of what Eco terms 'felicity conditions' to make a text 'fully actualized'. In *The*

Name of the Rose, Adso, who is the narrator and pupil of Brother William of Baskerville, asks William: 'To know what one book says you must read others?' William replies, 'At times this can be so. Often books speak of other books.' The novel articulates a sense of an ideal reader who can recognize the full range and play of references, allusions, parodies, and so on – just as Adso is being schooled in the reading of crime amongst other things by William, the actual reader aspires to a reading position which the text promotes.

The rise of the reader's importance in literary and critical theories has shifted the emphasis of criticism and interpretation away from author- and text-centred approaches to literature and has allowed for both a more plural set of responses to texts and also for more attention to the complex processes of reading and interpretation themselves. In one sense this shift can be seen as an ideological move away from author- and text-power to reader-power. In another way, it relocates literature as an historical product, subject to the context of consumption, recognizing that texts do change in relation to the circumstances in which they are read. The notions associated with author-centred or text-centred criticism of a singular, unified and 'correct' reading are no longer valid. Reader-response criticism and theory, and the related area of reception theory, will be considered in more detail later; it will also emerge as important in relation to psychoanalytical and feminist approaches. Perhaps it would be worth observing at this juncture that theory, far from removing literature from the individual reader or different reading groups, in fact restores the text and the reading 'experience' in ways which can now be discussed and explored explicitly: such approaches allow for an understanding of how meanings and different interpretations are generated and can help to dispel the sometimes authoritarian and intimidating attitudes that can arise in the teaching and study of literature. Theory is a powerful critical tool, and can itself be used in liberating or oppressive ways.

Notes

1 For fuller discussions of the rise of 'English' and its cultural and historical implications, see Chris Baldick, *The Social Mission of English Criticism* (Oxford, Oxford University Press, 1983); and Brian Doyle, 'The Invention of English', in Robert Colls and Philip Dodd, eds., *Englishness: Politics and Culture 1880–1920* (London, Croom Helm, 1986), pp. 89–115.

2 D.H. Lawrence, 'John Galsworthy', in A.A.H. Inglis, ed., *D.H. Lawrence: A Selection from Phoenix* (Harmondsworth, Penguin, 1971), p.284. First published in 1928.

3 F.R. Leavis, 'Literature and Society', in F.R. Leavis, *The Common Pursuit* (Harmondsworth, Penguin, 1976), p.194. First published in 1952.
4 T.S. Eliot, 'Tradition and the Individual Talent', in Frank Kermode, ed. *The Selected Prose of T.S. Eliot* (London, Faber & Faber, 1975), p.38. First published in 1919.
5 F.R. Leavis, 'Criticism and Philosophy', in Leavis *op. cit.*, pp.212–13.
6 See Terry Eagleton, *Literary Theory: An Introduction* (Oxford, Basil Blackwell, 1983), Chapter 1.
7 A.C. Bradley, *Oxford Lectures on Poetry* (London, Macmillan, 1950), pp.310–11. First published in 1909.
8 F.R. Leavis, 'The Irony of Swift', in Leavis, *op. cit.*, p.73.
9 Roland Barthes, 'The Death of the Author', in *Image-Music-Text* (London, Fontana, 1977), p.143. First published in France in 1968.
10 Michel Foucault, 'What is an Author?', in Jose V. Harari, ed., *Textual Strategies* (London, Methuen, 1980), pp. 141–60. First published in France in 1968.
11 For a discussion of the rise of biography in the nineteenth century and its impact on the formation of the discipline of English, see David Amigoni, *Victorian Biography: Intellectuals and the Ordering of Discourse* (Hemel Hempstead, Harvester, 1993).
12 Rene Wellek and Austin Warren, *Theory of Literature* (Harmondsworth, Penguin, 1973), p.42. First published in America in 1949.
13 Terry Eagleton, *op. cit.*, pp.120–1.
14 Roland Barthes, 'From Work to Text', in *op. cit.*, p. 161. First published in France in 1971.
15 Italo Calvino, *If on a winter's night a traveller* (London, Pan, 1982), p. 9. First published in Italy in 1979.

3 Language and narrative

This chapter examines two fundamental areas associated with the rise of literary and critical theory in Europe in the twentieth century and their more recent impact on literary criticism in Britain. Both of these may seem initially not to be of central importance as ways of thinking about literature. Certainly they depart from what we have called 'common sense' assumptions about both language and literature.

The starting point for such approaches has little to do with character and experience, but rather the raw materials of literary discourse: not so much what is described or represented but how these are constructed. They also are very different approaches from the kind of criticism advocated by Matthew Arnold, F.R. Leavis and their followers. The terminology and theoretical positions might seem more scientific in nature than to do with feeling and emotion, exactly what Leavis was opposed to, and rather different from the kind of approaches frequently encouraged in practical criticism sessions or in thinking about novels as equivalent to 'real life'. And in a sense, these new ideas might be characterized as scientific approaches in that they start from the position that literature is something knowable and definable rather than to do with affect and sensibility. *Language* is the basic material of literature in the broadest and narrowest senses of the category, and therefore should display particular characteristics which define its 'literariness' when we are dealing with literary discourse. *Narrative* is a way of looking at the organization and structuring of language into larger units, and though perhaps not as important in considering all kinds of poetry it is a very helpful way of looking at prose fiction and drama. We should not forget too that criticism and theory have their own kinds of language, and their own forms of narrative, at least when viewed from an historical perspective.

LANGUAGE

For many early literary critics, language was considered a secondary or passive medium for conveying ideas and experience. This kind of attitude is typified in a comment by W.J. Courthope, a nineteenth-century critic and Professor of Poetry at Oxford:

> Language is the instrument of thought, and like the winged sandals of Mercury, it may aid the mind to mount into the higher regions of thought and imagination. But it would be an error to take Mercury's sandals as the source of his divinity, and something of the kind would happen if, as might be done in the English school, the study of language were allowed to predominate over the study of literature.[1]

It is significant that Courthope sees 'thought' and 'imagination' as separate from language, and indeed that the study of literature is distinct from the study of language. In Britain in the twentieth century, language and literature have tended to be treated in rather separate ways in academic institutions. The study of language was mainly historical, that is looking at the evolution of the English language or concentrating on technical linguistic aspects of language. Neither of these approaches to language was closely integrated with the study of literature on the whole, and it was certainly possible to take a degree in 'English' at many institutions without having studied any language except in the context of practical criticism exercises which significantly do not depend on formal language theory.

In Europe in the early twentieth century various theories of language – and of literary language in particular – arose, which have had a profound impact on the study of literature in Britain since the late 1960s. I am not suggesting here that there have not been theories of language prior to the twentieth century which considered language as fundamental to literature, or which regarded language as the generator of ideas and meaning rather than as a medium for conveying these. Theories of rhetoric in ancient Greece, and the nineteenth-century American C.S. Pierce's work on language, precede the following theories. It has been suggested that rhetoric might well be resurrected as a relevant model for literary study by Terry Eagleton in *Literary Theory: An Introduction* (1983) where he makes a strong case for this in his conclusion. However, the early twentieth century does constitute a particular historical 'moment' in the way that language and subsequently literary theory have been rethought, and the work of Saussure in particular is fundamental to the growth of what has become known as structuralism, a concept which embraces a much broader field of knowledge than literary study.

The theory of the sign

The work of the Swiss linguist Ferdinand de Saussure (1857–1913) challenged the assumption that language was a 'natural' phenomenon, just 'there' in effect. It had been argued in the nineteenth century that language was natural in the sense that it fitted the worlds of objects and ideas through its sound patterns and structures, that there was a right word for every aspect of the world. Some theologians also turned their attention to the origins and meaning of language, such as Archbishop Trench, who in *The Study of Words* (1851) provided explanations to many terms which were supposedly God given. In contrast, Saussure suggested that language is an *arbitrary* and *conventional* system. By arbitrary, he meant that there is no inherently natural reason why the word 'dog' should mean what it does. In other languages the same object is described by quite unrelated words: 'hund' in German and 'chien' in French for example. Even onomatopoeic words – where the sound is supposed to imitate the noise – change from country to country. By conventional, Saussure meant that language is a sign system or code whose conventions are agreed by a particular society so that communication can take place. Learning a language is to participate in these conventions, which may vary in both vocabulary and grammatical structure from language to language.

According to Saussure, the production of meaning is the result of a process of combination and selection within a language system which functions through the generation and recognition of differences. We come to recognize, for example, that 'dog' is different from 'cat' through the different meanings or signifieds attached to the different sounds or signifiers. He identifies two axes which contribute to this process: the *syntagmatic* axis and the *paradigmatic* axis. Meaning is produced along the syntagmatic axis, as in the sentence through the accumulation of its component parts: 'I / read / a / book / yesterday.' The meaning of this sentence could be extended along the syntagmatic axis, for example: 'I read a good book yesterday', or ' I read a good book yesterday evening', and so on. If however we were to extend the meaning in another direction, for example, 'I read an obscene book yesterday in hospital', then such changes which operate by association operate along the paradigmatic axis; this is achieved without reference to any extra-linguistic reality.

Saussure divided up the concept of language into two areas which have subsequently been very important in literary theory: *langue* and *parole*. By langue, he meant the totality of language: its entire vocabulary and grammar. By parole, he indicated a particular utterance or 'speech act' which draws on and combines various elements from the langue aspect. A sonnet or a joke would be examples of rather different kinds of parole. Most varieties of literary criticism have tended to concentrate on literature as parole – as a distinctive and unique piece of writing – without thinking about how such a work is related to or different from more conventional writing and from langue or language as a whole. As we shall see in the following section, 'Literary language', following on from Saussure some literary theorists addressed this question of the 'literariness' of literary language or discourse as distinct from other kinds of language. Saussure's work has been criticized for taking a rather ahistorical view of language: for example Diane Macdonnell in *Theories of Discourse* (1986) argues that : 'Saussure's linguistics used a humanist notion of society, and supposed that anything social was homogeneous and held in common by everyone', and that such linguistics 'evacuated history and change'. There is a tendency to see language as in itself absolute and uncontested even if each language system is arbitrary and conventional in its composition, but arguably Saussure's work does emphasize both the historical dimension of language and its potential for change and conflict in his emphasis on the *synchronic* (parole) and *diachronic* (langue), both of which can be used to illustrate his awareness of time in relation to language and that meaning is conditional on historical situations. The concept of parole might be seen as suggesting that each speech act will be different not only according to its formal properties but also according to the historical conditions in which it is produced. Later theorists though have viewed language with more historical emphasis than in the formal or structural terms which Saussure introduced. This does not invalidate the fundamental contribution and impact of Saussure's work in allowing for very different ways of thinking about language, and as a founding figure of structuralism.

The most important feature of Saussure's work is the theory of the *sign*. Saussure saw all language systems as composed of various signs to which a concept or an image is attached by association. Thus we come to recognize that the sound *d-o-g* means a four-legged hairy mammal and is different from the sounds *m-a-t* or *h-a-t* which in turn have different meanings attached to them, and so on. Language is for Saussure a twofold or binary system; such a system consists of a code which is conveyed through verbal or visual signs which have agreed concepts or meanings attached. This distinction is expressed by the following related terms: *signifier* and *signified.* The signifier is the particular sound or phonetic configuration which produces the word 'dog' and the signified the concept or image associated with it. Language is thus a system of differences: as Saussure said, 'in language there are only differences'. It is this structure of differences in terms of sounds and their related meanings which for Saussure constitutes the way that we know and understand the world, and which appealed to later theorists, in particular those which are generally labelled as structuralists and poststructuralists. It is noticeable that these theorists, who have exerted such a profound influence on twentieth-century thinking, see 'reality' in terms of underlying structures and forces. Their ideas displace the apparently autonomous individual, freethinking and acting subject of humanism – often significantly called 'man' – from the central position he hitherto seemed to occupy as the source and originator of meaning. Instead of people shaping language to their own ends, the implication of Saussure's theories led to the idea that people are shaped or determined by language; as the German philosopher Martin Heidegger stated, 'language speaks us'. People are born into language in effect: James Joyce's character Stephen Dedalus in *A Portrait of the Artist as a Young Man* (1916) illustrates this point well as he is brought up through the discourses of religion, politics, family and education, the 'nets' of language as Joyce calls them, and tries to escape to forge his own language as an expression of his own identity.

For Saussure language is essentially a social and not an individual phenomenon. The very shared, communicative aspect of language makes this necessarily so:

> The arbitrary nature of the sign explains in turn why the social fact alone can create a linguistic system. The community is necessary if values that owe their existence solely to usage and general acceptance are to be set up; by himself the individual is incapable of fixing a single value.[2]

Language then is 'natural' not in the sense of its being naturally available as a way of describing the world, but through social usage and familiarity: it becomes a naturalized process or activity. Language may give the illusion of being transparent and referential – of referring to a world beyond itself – but the implications of Saussure's theories are that language constructs the sense of the world as we know it. One striking feature of language in many contexts is its ability not to draw attention to itself as language. As we shall see, some literary theorists have suggested that a feature of literary or poetic language is its self-consciousness, foregrounding its own status as language. More generally, though not as apparent as in say experimental Modernist poetry or Shakespearian drama, language can be said to signify or construct the world rather than passively reflecting it. It would appear to be the case that the relationship of objects in the world is the same as the relationships in language which represent that world, but, following Saussure, it can be argued that language confers these relationships on to what we take to be the world existing outside of or independently from language.

The view of language as a social and collective phenomenon following certain conventions would seem to conflict with the notion that it is at the same time suited to the expression of highly individual, original and imaginative ideas – as is certainly the case with more romantic views of the literary artist. We have already seen how the idea of the 'author' has been questioned and redefined according to certain literary theorists. Saussure allows us to look at language in a more structured and scientific way so that what might otherwise be thought of as the author's mind and imagination could now be addressed as language: the uniqueness of a literary text could be seen in its formal linguistic properties rather than by delving into the author's life and background. But it also lets us think of writing as something which is, to use Saussure's terminology, a *parole* arising out of the *langue*; that is a particular or specific text which is related to the general system and conventions of language. Now linguists and literary theorists have sought to redefine Saussure's categories of langue and parole, but this view does allow us to think of literature in relation to other forms of language, and also to ask what does constitute the uniqueness or originality of literary discourse: how far can the parole remove itself from the conventions of langue? Or, to use Saussure's concept of language as difference, how far does or can literary discourse differ from other kinds of 'normal' language?

In concluding this section on the theory of the sign, it is worth mentioning that Saussure's theories, first published posthumously in 1914 under the title *Course in General Linguistics,* were not written directly by Saussure but were compiled from notes taken from his lectures in Paris by students and friends. This highlights appropriately one of the implications of the theories attributed to Saussure: are we dealing with views which are the product of one individual and which existed prior to and outside of the language in which they are expressed, or rather a more collective 'social' text which is itself a reflection on language?

Literary language

Saussure's theories pointed the way for a rethinking of the nature of language and formed part of a much broader movement which was particularly evident in linguistic philosophy. It is worth mentioning briefly that some philosophers at this time, such as Ludwig Wittgenstein, felt that the great questions which philosophy had traditionally addressed about the meaning of life and so on were in effect questions about language, though not usually perceived as such. However, in the context of literature, linguists and critics began to ask whether literature might be identifiable by its linguistic characteristics. Rather than thinking about special kinds of experience and moral values as English critics had traditionally done, a group of East European critics formulated a series of arguments about the nature of literary language. These arguments could well be described as the first examples of modern literary theory and their proponents (where they can be identified, in the case of some Russian writers) the first modern literary theorists who have greatly influenced the work of more recent theorists in France especially and subsequently in America and Britain. Indeed, much of their work has only been translated and widely circulated since the 1960s. What is particularly striking in historical terms is to contrast the conceptions of the 'literary' and the role or function of literature which emerge from these theorists with those that were commonly held in Britain at the same time. Perhaps we should note too that literary criticism, and literary and critical theory, are as much involved in, and products of, historical processes as are the literary texts which they address.

Literary language and 'literariness'

The main theories about the nature of literature in terms of its linguistic characteristics derive from a group which arose in Russia in 1915 and whose members are now usually referred to as the Russian Formalists. The term 'formalism' here should not be confused with the critical movement which goes under the same name which arose in America in the 1940s and 1950s which is also often referred to as formalism as well as New Criticism. The interests of Russian Formalism are rather different from the narrow textual approach advocated by the New Critics within their version of formalism, and much closer to the developments in literary theory beginning in the 1960s.

Victor Shklovsky and 'defamiliarization'

Shklovsky was one of the most important members of the Moscow Linguistic Circle and in 1917 published an essay called 'Art as Technique'. In this Shklovsky introduced a concept which in translation has become known as *defamiliarization*. His thesis was that in most activities perception becomes a habitual, automatic process where we are often unaware of, or take for granted our view of things and the relations between them. Poetic, or literary, language could disturb this 'habitualization' and make us see things differently and anew. This is achieved by the ability of poetic or literary language to 'make strange' or defamiliarize the familiar world; what changed in fact was not the world or object in question but the way of perceiving it: the mode of perception:

> And art exists that one may recover the sensation of life; it exists to make one feel things, to make the stone *stony*. The purpose of art is to impart the sensation of things as they are perceived and not as they are known. The technique of art is to make objects *'unfamiliar'*, to make forms difficult, to increase the difficulty and the length of perception because the process of perception is an aesthetic end in itself and must be prolonged. *Art is a way of experiencing the artfulness of an object; the object is not important.*[3]

Now clearly not all literature has this effect of defamiliarization; many nineteenth- and twentieth-century novels for example seem to do the very opposite and reinforce the world as we seem to know it by using language which is not strange or inaccessible but creates a sense of familiarity and recognition. Shklovsky's theory is helpful in understanding experimental writing, in particular that which has become known as Modernism which was at its height when his essay was published. The poetry of Ezra Pound or T.S. Eliot can certainly be said to have such an effect as can, in different ways, the prose fiction of James Joyce's *Ulysses* (1922) or Franz Kafka's *Metamorphosis* (1916). Modernism does emphasize form rather than content, and everyday events such as walking down a street or waking up become radically transformed in these literary texts. Shklovsky acknowledges though that defamiliarization effects will change over time, so that one generation's defamiliarization will become the next generation's habituation or norm. But what Shklovsky's theory also shows is that all versions of reality are constructed, though not so self-consciously or subversively as those which employ such defamiliarization devices. The realist novel because of its recycling of habitual language and the processes of perception thus involved establishes itself as natural and normal, but this too is an effect. The playwright Bertolt Brecht developed these ideas into a form of dramatic practice which foregrounded the constructed nature of realist drama by constantly disrupting the smooth surface of the action to interject comments and other kinds of actions; what Brecht called his *'verfremdungseffekte'* or *alienation effect* is equivalent to Shklovsky's concept of defamiliarization, forcing the audience to see the action from different perspectives and making their position in relation to the text less obvious or naturalized. In *The Life of Galileo* (1938–47) for example, Brecht indicates in his 'Author's Notes' on the play that:

> the characterization of Galileo should not aim at establishing a sympathetic identification and participation of the audience with him; rather, the audience should be helped to achieve a more considering, critical and appraising attitude. He should be presented as a phenomenon, rather like Richard III, whereby the audience's emotional acceptance is gained through the vitality of this alien manifestation.[4]

One of Brecht's techniques was to draw attention to character as character – as a constructed device or effect in the dramatic text, to make the actors distance themselves from their roles so that their performance becomes a critical reflection on the character rather than a portrayal which strives for realism which consequently diminishes the emphasis on a character's formation through social and historical forces.

Shklovsky's theory offers an alternative to the views which would see literature as a repository for timeless and universal values and truths: instead literariness is a linguistic effect produced in a particular context in relation to other kinds of knowledge or discourse. It also moves towards the view that literature or a literary text is not ultimately unified and organic in nature but rather composed of various kinds of writings, techniques or devices which can be assembled and interpreted in various ways. A revealing case study in this respect would be Coleridge's poem 'Kubla Khan' (1816). There have been many attempts to 'explain' the poem in terms of the author, including Coleridge's own postscript, or in terms of period and so on. But a reading of the poem which looks closely at its linguistic features and compares them with more conventional kinds of discourse both from the period of composition and from that of the period in which it is read, would reveal the highly unusual and experimental use of sound, syntax and vocabulary which produces the range of effects more often put down to the 'imagination'. This kind of approach also allows for more varied and plural responses than an attempt to close the poem

...d a particular aspect such as the writer, the location, or claims
...rding the potential organic unity of the poem itself.

Bakhtin/Volosinov and 'the dialogic'

Mikhail Bakhtin was also associated with the Moscow Linguistic
Circle and went on to develop theories of literary language which have
been highly influential in recent years. There is some ambiguity as to
the identity of Mikhail Bakhtin, or at least the authorship of some of
his writings which have been published under the name of V.N.
Volosinov, who was an associate of Bakhtin. The debate over authorship has not been finally resolved, but the texts published under either
Bakhtin or Volosinov share a common theoretical framework and,
bearing in mind our earlier discussion on the figure of the author, it
might be more profitable to see these writings as part of a common
discursive practice rather than raise unnecessary and diversionary
questions about authorship and the attendant issues of 'authority'
which Bakhtin/Volosinov were attempting to expose.

Although Bakhtin concurred with Saussure in that he saw language
as fundamental to all meaning and the raw material of knowledge, he
differed from him in that he considered language as a social and
historical process rather than an abstract and unified system as implied
in Saussure's term 'langue'. Language for Bakhtin is not in any sense
fixed or stable but always in a state of flux; meaning is never singular
and uncontested but rather plural and contested. At the most basic
level, any act of communication is potentially open to at least two
interpretations: that of the speaker/writer and that of the listener/
reader, so that if I say 'I believe in the freedom of the individual', these
words will presumably have at least one meaning for me but may have
other meanings for the person who is addressed, dependent on a range
of conditions. They will probably be further modified if they are read
by a range of people, especially if this occurs over a period of years.
For Bakhtin language is not in any sense 'arbitrary', nor is it consensual: rather it constitutes a site for struggle so that when the word
'freedom' is used, for example, it has no clear cut meaning but can
have entirely different, even opposed significances for different people and social groups. As used, for example, by political parties in
Britain in the 1980s, the word can have a range of meanings, some of
which are quite contradictory. This, of course, is a different matter
than Saussure's 'arbitrary system' of matching sound to object.

This potential in language to mean different things Bakhtin termed
dialogic; the term is obviously linked to the idea of dialogue in that it

implies language is a two way or multiple process rather than as a unitary phenomenon, which is the tendency in Saussure's theories. Bakhtin's general view of language is as a field of struggle between what he calls the 'centripetal' or *monologic* forces which strive to impose a singular, fixed meaning and the 'centrifugal' or *dialogic* forces which contest or fragment the singular into plural or multiple meanings. According to Bakhtin, we find throughout western history attempts to '*unify and centralize the verbal-ideological world*', but:

> Alongside the centripetal forces, the centrifugal forces of language carry on their uninterrupted work; alongside verbal-ideological centralization and unification, the uninterrupted processes of decentralization and disunification go forward.[5]

Although all language is inherently dialogic, Bakhtin argued that in certain kinds of writing this is more pronounced and evident than in others. In particular, literary language displays a high index of dialogism, and for Bakhtin the novel displays the 'many-voicedness' or *heteroglossia* which reveals the full play of meanings potentially available in language. For Bakhtin the novel is composed of multiple layers of discourse which align themselves in various ways, some harmonious and others oppositional. What the novel allows for is the challenging and subverting of monologic and authoritarian discourse by other kinds of language which parody or deflate the central, official language and values. This is linked to Bakhtin's concept of the 'carnivalesque' whereby literature can draw on discourses outside the established language of authority to suspend the 'hierarchical structure and all the forms of terror, reverence, piety, and etiquette connected with it'. Carnival permits people who in life are 'separated by impenetrable hierarchical barriers [to] enter into free and familiar contact', thus suspending the established official order and allowing new relationships to emerge. For Bakhtin, carnival is essentially ambivalent and 'dualistic', recognizing and encouraging dialogic relations quite openly.

The novel may arrange its many discourses in different ways, so that typically in the realist text there is a clear hierarchy of discourses controlled by a privileged central voice or narrator whereas the Modernist text has no such centralized voice but rather presents a free play of voices none of which is clearly privileged. Nevertheless, novels generally by their very nature draw on a variety of discourses which involve potential realignments of language and social relations. An obvious and rather literal illustration of Bakhtin's theories would be

Dickens's *Hard Times* where the official discourses of education, industrialization, marriage and wealth are set against the discourses of the circus and Sissy Jupe. The descriptions of Coketown emphasize the monotonous mechanical aspect of industrialization, but these are juxtaposed with defamiliarizing metaphorical language which undermines the authoritarian and utilitarian discourses:

> Coketown, to which Messrs Bounderby and Gradgrind now walked, was a triumph of fact; it had no greater taint of fancy than Mrs Gradgrind herself. Let us strike the keynote, Coketown, before pursuing our tune.
>
> It was a town of red brick, or brick that would have been red if the smoke and ashes had allowed it; but, as matters stood it was a town of unnatural red and black like the painted face of a savage. It was a town of machinery and tall chimneys, out of which interminable serpents of smoke trailed themselves for ever and ever, and never got uncoiled. It had a black canal in it, and a river that ran purple with ill-smelling dye, and vast piles of building full of windows where there was a rattling and trembling all day long, and where the piston of the steam-engine worked monotonously up and down, like the head of an elephant in a state of melancholy madness.[6]

Although the spheres of officialdom are not completely overthrown, they are modified and a more tolerant resolution is negotiated: a strategy much favoured in nineteenth-century realist fiction.

The implications of Bakhtin's theories for literature, language and literary criticism are very significant. Rather than literature being a timeless, universal and stable body of knowledge it is subject to change and different, even antithetical readings may emerge. In the same way language is no longer a unified, homogeneous and abstract system, but heterogeneous and 'material' in that it constitutes knowledge and consciousness. Insofar as literary criticism is concerned, we can view it too as a form of language or discourse which has its own dialogic characteristics and which is subject to historical conditions. We might view the relationship of some literary criticism to literature as one of competing discourses, seeking to establish certain 'truths' and close off other readings in much the same way that a privileged voice can operate in the realist novel, making the reader see things in a certain way from a particular point of view which is constructed as natural or universal. Bakhtin's theories encourage a more plural and interrogative response to literature than some critics and institutions have wanted to recognize.

Roland Barthes has developed Bakhtin's ideas about language, arguing that language which draws attention to itself as language –

what he calls the 'double' sign which, whilst conveying a sense of meaning, also conveys a sense of how that meaning is produced – is more healthy than that which disguises itself and passes itself off as 'natural' thus masking the signifying process. This approach combines Bakhtin's concept of the dialogic and Shklovsky's concept of defamiliarization, both dedicated to subverting the 'obvious'.

Jakobson and 'metaphor and metonymy'

Roman Jakobson was another figure associated with the Moscow Linguistic Circle. He later joined the Prague Linguistic Circle of the 1920s and 1930s, and subsequently moved to America where, as in Britain, his theories have been influential in literary and critical theory.

Jakobson had wide interests in language and linguistics which went beyond the literary, and his work is also important in psychiatry in terms of theories of language disturbance or deviance in mental illness. Indeed, issues regarding linguistic disturbance or deviance are the basis of Jakobson's main theories on language and literariness. For Jakobson, language as a whole can be divided into two main categories, or rather certain kinds of language tend to exhibit characteristics which locate them towards one or other of two linguistic axes or poles which Jakobson identifies: what he terms *metaphor* on the one hand and *metonymy* on the other. Jakobson's poles of language are derived from clinical observations of psychiatric patients suffering from 'aphasia' or speech disturbance, the conclusions of which were published in an essay called 'Two Aspects of Language and Two Types of Aphasic Disturbance' (1956). The terms *metaphor* and *metonymy* refer to figures of speech and Jakobson extends these categories to encompass wider features of language common to particular kinds of writing or discourse. *Metonymy* is the less well-known term which strictly means to substitute the name of an attribute for the thing meant, for example 'crown' for the 'monarch' or 'hands' for 'sailors'. *Metaphor* on the other hand is the application of a name or term to an object to which it is not literally applicable, for example 'a skeleton crew' where a word taken from anatomy is used to create a sharpened image of a small and inadequate ship's crew. In the passage quoted above from *Hard Times,* the metaphor 'serpents of smoke' and the metaphorical effect of the similes 'like the painted face of a savage' and 'like the head of an elephant in a state of melancholy madness' are juxtaposed with following descriptions of the houses, streets and people, the latter usually reduced to 'hands', which are predominantly metonymical in character creating an effect of sameness, of a monotonous and undifferentiated existence. The metaphors also tend to animate in grotesque ways the inanimate, mechanical features of Coketown whereas its inhabitants are de-animated as part of the dehumanizing effects of industrialization.

As a result of observing patients suffering from aphasia, Jakobson identified two kinds of language or speech disturbance. The first he called 'similarity disorder' in which patients became stuck in a chain of language which it was impossible to break out of although words from within a particular chain might be displaced by another, e.g. 'knife' for 'fork' or 'blade' for 'knife'. Patients suffering from similarity disorder were also unable to use language in abstract or unliteral ways, so that they could not say 'It's raining' if it was not actually raining. Jakobson likened this kind of disturbance to the metonymic aspect of language where a discourse is characterized by its relationships of similarity through association.

The second form of aphasia Jakobson called 'contiguity disorder' in which the speech of patients appeared to make little or no sense because the relationships normally existing between words were violently disrupted. The language of people thus affected could appear completely random and disorganized. This kind of aphasic disturbance Jakobson likened to the metaphoric aspect of language in that the use of metaphor is a form of linguistic disturbance in which a word from one linguistic chain or field will be transplanted into another in order to heighten the meaning.

Jakobson went on to suggest that certain forms of writing – literary and other kinds of language – tend towards either the metonymic or metaphoric poles. Realism or documentary, for example, exhibit highly metonymic qualities whereas modernist and experimental fiction and poetry are more dislocated and thus more metaphoric in quality. Some texts may combine elements from both these axes: an example would be *King Lear* (1606) where the play opens in metonymic mode with the language of kingship and paternal authority and established social order, and Lear invokes a higher, metaphysical chain of being: 'For, by the sacred radiance of the sun, / The mysteries of Hecate and the night, / By all the operation of the orbs / From whom we do exist and cease to be. ... ' As Lear's family, court and personality fragment so his language shifts into a very disturbed and metaphoric style, which climaxes in the storm scene:

Poor naked wretches, whereso'er you are,
That bide the pelting of this pitiless storm,

How shall your houseless heads and unfed sides,
Your loop'd and window'd raggedness, defend you
From such seasons as these? O! I have ta'en
Too little care of this. Take Physic, Pomp;
Expose thyself to feel what wretches feel,
That thou mayst shake the superflux to them,
And show the Heavens more just.[7]

Metaphor is arguably a more innovative and productive mode, capable of generating different or new meanings in ways that metonymic language cannot, the latter being more concerned with reinforcing familiar patterns of understanding. This is so not only at the level of meaning or signification, but also with structure or syntax, so that the steady balanced periodic sentence would be linked to metonymy and more dislocated structures – even to the extent of abandoning punctuation, as for example in the poetry of e.e. cummings or some of James Joyce's or William Faulkner's prose fiction – would be related to metaphor.

The other relevant theory of literary language which Jakobson developed was concerned with a category he termed the *poetic*. By this, he meant that poetic or literary language is different from other forms of writing in that it 'thickens' and draws attention to itself, an argument not far removed from some of the ideas about literary language which we have already looked at. Related to this is Jakobson's concept of the *dominant*: that is, various forms of writing or genres, and within these specific texts, display particularly dominant linguistic features. Another way of looking at this is that a text *foregrounds* certain aspects of language: that is, certain linguistic features are emphasized or stressed. Poetry in general foregrounds sound or the phonetic aspect of language in ways that are not common to other genres. Within poetry, certain phonetic arrangements allow us to identify particular kinds of poetic form combined with certain structural foregrounding, so that we come to recognize a sonnet as distinct from a ballad, and so on. Realist or documentary writing will foreground referential language, that is language which appears to refer to an external world beyond itself, whereas what has become known as metafictional writing foregrounds its own language and constructed nature rather than an apparent world outside language. Just as a text has certain *dominant* characteristics, there is also the aspect of *deviance* – those linguistic features which break from the conventions of the dominant. A good illustration of this would be George Orwell's documentary writing, for example *The Road to*

Wigan Pier (1937), where occasionally the narrative departs from referential metonymic language to the metaphoric axis. In the following passage, there is a noticeable shift from the documentary descriptive conventions which Orwell establishes in the text to a more poetic, literary and metaphoric mode, which parallels the movement from an industrial to a rural landscape:

> In a crowded, dirty little country like ours one takes defilement almost for granted. Slag-heaps and chimneys seem a more normal, probable landscape than grass and trees, and even in the depths of the country you half expect to lever up a broken bottle or a rusty can. But out here the snow was untrodden and lay so deep that only the tops of the stone boundary-walls were showing, winding over the hills like black paths. I remembered that D.H. Lawrence, writing of this same landscape or another near by, said that the snow-covered hills rippled away into the distance 'like muscle'. It was not the simile that would have occurred to me. To my eye the snow and the black walls were more like a white dress with black piping running across it.[8]

Jakobson's theories have been criticized for being too formalistic in emphasis, not taking full account of the historical dimension of language. Certainly *metaphor* and *metonymy* are not 'fixed' categories: language changes so that metaphors become ingrained and 'normal' once they have lost their innovative force, indeed they can become clichés and thus reinforce the familiar rather than offering unfamiliar images. Jakobson's concept of the *poetic* and foregrounding also implies that literary language is a deviation from the norm. This has been questioned by some theorists who have argued that there is no such thing as 'normal' language – and indeed some have further argued that all language is inherently metaphorical – so that literary language is not necessarily different from other forms of discourse. Certainly I think it is dangerous to have rigid categories and boundaries as to literary and non-literary discourse. Literary discourse is a *relative* category both formally and historically and thus liable to change and open to redefinition. Its formal characteristics emerge by differentiation from other kinds of language, and its historical nature by differentiation from – or compliance with – official and conventional discourses. It would be unhelpful and inaccurate to suggest, as some critics have, that literary language is an entirely subjective phenomenon, in the eye of the beholder so to speak, which would ignore the larger social and ideological aspects of language and literary discourse. But on the other hand the concept of literature and 'literariness' is a contested area and thus subject to redefinition, not an objective and unchanging area in terms of language any more than morality or 'truthfulness'. The traditional artistic notions of originality or the more modern concept of 'make it new' both imply that literature defines itself by difference, by innovation, and thus literary criticism and theory might be expected to shift their ground to engage with such departures from established conventions.

Perhaps a more profitable approach to adopt is to see all forms of writing, all texts, as employing various devices of language and narrative which seek to establish certain kinds of knowledge and validity. These devices vary immensely, from those which we are very familiar with – indeed possibly so familiar that we fail to see them as devices, to those which are unusual, complex and problematic. To focus attention solely on literary texts in this way diverts attention from the forms of textuality which surround us continuously, and which may indeed display literary qualities or have complexities and subtleties equivalent to the 'literary' which have been ignored or dismissed because of the way in which 'literature' has been traditionally viewed or constructed. Attempts to fix literary language through a refined vocabulary (e.g. the *poetic* diction favoured by many poets in the eighteenth century) result in a closed and eventually stale form of writing. It is essential for critics to be aware of the kinds of language in circulation at the moment of production and consumption of texts and to be able to 'read' these according to their historical significance. Clearly texts change through history, and the main reason for their changing is the way that language works. Certain kinds of literary language are at the margins of conventional discourse, pushing meaning to its limits in a particular historical moment. But literature is capable of modifying knowledge, of opening up the closed and unitary or monologic language of official or conventional discourse. For example, in William Blake's poem 'London' from *Songs of Experience* (1794), the opening line 'I wander thro' each charter'd street', the word 'charter'd' can signify two quite different meanings. 'Charter'd' in the sense of Royal Charters and guarantees of liberty, but also 'charter'd' in the senses of to hire and to limit, suggesting that liberty is not what it appears to be. Literary language can shift the stable *signifier* towards new or multiple *signifieds*.

NARRATIVE

Together with language, narrative has been one of the most important areas for modern literary theory. Studies of narrative in the twentieth century, especially those originating in Europe, are fundamental to 'structuralism' and have extended beyond the analysis of literary texts into wider cultural and anthropological fields.[9] Narrative can seem so obvious or natural that we can overlook its significance: it can just seem to be 'there' like language – transparent or invisible. On the other hand, critics or theorists from Aristotle onwards have been aware of narrative as the fundamental and essential substance of literary texts, whether dramatic, fictional or poetic, although some poetry displays fewer narrative characteristics than most fiction or drama does. For Aristotle, a play had a beginning, a middle and an end; he also identified more complex characteristics in classical Greek drama such as *peripeteia* where the action undergoes a reversal or change in direction. In Britain and America the importance of the novel as an object of study in the twentieth century was accompanied by a growth in novel criticism and the beginnings of theories of fiction. Henry James's 'Prefaces' to his novels drew attention to his belief that the significance of the form in which a story is told was more crucial than the subject of the story, and he developed the term 'post of observation' which later became refined into *point of view* and more recently has been theorized as narrative *focalization*. In *Aspects of the Novel* (1927), E.M. Forster made the distinction between 'story' and 'plot' which has also been developed in more recent narrative theory, which is explained later in this section.

Narrative and language can be seen as mutually inclusive aspects of literary texts or discourse. Narrative is a way of combining units of language into larger structures, and virtually all uses of language involve or imply a sense of time, direction and action. One of the fundamental conditions of narrative is a 'teller' and a 'listener' or 'reader': figures that pass under a variety of terms. Roman Jakobson in his 'communication model' calls them the *addresser* and the *addressee*, terms which cover the entire range of different kinds of narrator and narratee. Narrative units can be formed from the simplest through to the most complicated of linguistic combinations and operations. For two recent literary theorists, narrative is the necessary, inevitable condition of language, meaning and knowledge. Roland Barthes in his essay 'Introduction to the Structural Analysis of Narratives' (1966) expresses it thus:

> The narratives of the world are numberless. Narrative is first and foremost a prodigious variety of genres, themselves distributed amongst different substances – as though any material were fit to receive man's stories. Able to be carried by articulated language, spoken or written, fixed or moving images, gestures, and the ordered mixture of all these substances; narrative

is present in myth, legend, fable, tale, novella, epic, history, tragedy, drama, comedy, mime, painting, (think of Carpaccio's *Saint Ursula*), stained glass windows, cinema, comics, news item, conversation. Moreover, under this almost infinite diversity of forms, narrative is present in every age, in every place, in every society; it begins with the very history of mankind and there nowhere is or has been a people without narrative ... Caring nothing for the division between good or bad literature, narrative is international, trans-historical, transcultural: it is simply there, like life itself.[10]

The American critic and theorist Fredric Jameson talks of 'the all-informing process of *narrative*, which I take to be ... the central function or instance of the human mind.'[11]

Narrative is thus considered to underpin or structure all our writing and thinking: all forms of knowledge. As with language, we might expect there to be certain elements which narratives have in common with each other, but also that narratives are distinctive and distinguishable through differentiation. What makes *Great Expectations* (1862) different from *Bleak House* (1852–3)? How can we see a more obvious difference between these and Agatha Christie's *The Murder of Roger Ackroyd* (1926), and understand that the novels by Dickens also share certain properties which make them in more conventional terms recognizable as works by the same author? The tension between similarity or convention and difference is very much at the centre of narrative theory and helps to account for the ways in which we classify and organize different forms of writing to which we assign various kinds and hierarchies of knowledge and truth.

Narratology: narrative and narration

The study of theories of narrative has become known as narratology: effectively the grammar of narrative. As with language, the first modern theories of narrative derive from early twentieth-century Russia and the movement known as Russian Formalism. Rather later Roland Barthes was to ask the question of how it might be possible to classify narratives and produce a 'model' which would serve to illustrate the main characteristics of narrative. Barthes saw two possible ways of doing this. Either the inductive method is employed in which all narratives, or as many as feasible, are surveyed and their features noted. Or the deductive method is employed in which a hypothetical model or theory is propounded and then tested against various narratives.

The first major attempt to produce a 'model' for narrative had in fact combined both approaches in that it involved the survey of nearly

200 examples of a particular narrative genre, the folk-tale, which after an analysis of its constituent elements might then be broadened to apply to other narrative forms. This was undertaken by the Russian Formalist Vladimir Propp, and the findings published in *Morphology of the Folk-Tale* (1928). The folk-tale was composed of seven 'spheres of action' and thirty-one constant 'functions' or elements. Each individual folk-tale used various permutations of the these: the 'spheres of action' are the figures which tend to predominate in such tales, for example the hero, the villain, the helper, the lost figure, and so on. The 'functions' are the events or actions which drive the narrative on in a certain direction. Propp's findings are that not all the thirty-one functions need to recur in each narrative, but those which are selected always occur in the same order. The tales end with the marriage 'function' in Propp's scheme, though not always a literal marriage but variations such as the acquiring of wealth or the return to a unified family. What is important about Propp's work is not that it provides a complete understanding of narrative – in fact this is far from the case as folk-tales are usually simple, linear narratives – but that he points to the underlying or immanent pattern or structure of narrative in a particular genre. The material which Propp is working on inevitably restricts the scope of his analysis, and the analysis itself concentrates on the linear or horizontal aspect of narrative and does not move to consider the integrative or vertical aspect of narrative where higher complexities of structure and meaning arise. At the interpretive level, Propp sees the 'desire' aspect of narrative as highly significant, and reads the 'marriage' endings in which the desire for an object is gratified (e.g. a princess or a pot of gold) as metaphors for the Russian peasant's desire for food. What Propp does not explain so easily is the endings which depart from this pattern and have no neat resolution. Nevertheless, Propp's work results in an early attempt to theorize narrative and draws attention to its constructed nature; character for example is seen more as a device or function for holding together the action rather than being equivalent to 'real' people doing 'real' things.

There have been many developments leading on from Propp, some of which have taken a more structuralist approach to narrative than others. Roland Barthes sees the process of narrative as reducible to two elements or functions: what he terms 'catalysers' and 'nuclei'. Catalysers play a kind of background or incidental role whereas nuclei are 'hinge-points' of the narrative where there are crucial moments of development or integration which 'inaugurate or conclude an uncertainty'. Thus in *Great Expectations* the meeting between Pip and

Magwitch at the opening of the novel would act as a nuclei, as would the eventual revelation that Magwitch is Pip's true benefactor and Estella's father. In Agatha Christie's *The Murder of Roger Ackroyd* the dictation voice-recording machine may appear to perform initially the function of a catalyser in that it appears to have a simply passive role contributing to the novel's realism, but as the narrative is eventually untangled it assumes the status of a nuclei as a significant agent in the murder plot; detective or thriller novels often play with narrative units by concealing their full significance until the mystery is finally unravelled. Barthes' overall theory of narrative is complex and needs to be studied in detail; it builds on the work of Propp and others in revealing the immanent aspects of narrative so that it becomes difficult to read a text and to remain at a 'surface' level of interpretation in relation to plot and narrative significance.

It could be argued that the theories of narrative propounded by Propp and Barthes are more concerned with the analysis of 'content': that is of character, action and setting. Narratives operate not only at the level of stories about characters, events and places, but also at the level of their telling or *narration*. Traditional criticism would have used the terms 'content' and 'form' to differentiate between these aspects of a text, the content being the substance of the narrative and the form the way in which that substance is presented. More recently, this distinction has been given various terms as narrative theory has developed. The French theorist Gérard Genette in *Narrative Discourse* (1972) makes the distinction between '*histoire*' or *story*, '*récit*' or *narrative*, and '*narration*' or *narrating*. Through these terms, Genette further breaks down narrative into its constituent parts and places particular emphasis on textuality and the process of telling or narrating itself. By *histoire/story* is meant the story as a succession of events, what Genette calls the 'narrative content'. If we take *Wuthering Heights* (1847) as an illustration, then it is the linear story – the characters and events in that novel – which we could summarize if we had to say what the novel is 'about'; Genette also likens this to Saussure's concept of the *signified*. By *récit/narrative*, the actual text is meant, the spoken or written language or discourse which articulates the story and which may rearrange the order of events and present characters in various relations to each other which are not complete in the 'story' sense; Genette sees this as equivalent to Saussure's category of the signifier. Thus in *Wuthering Heights*, the action is not presented chronologically, but in a dislocated temporal scheme; we also do not get a full sense of Heathcliff until we assemble all the various accounts of his character. By *narration/narrating* the level of the actual telling of the story and narrative is indicated, what Genette calls 'the producing of the narrative action'. Again, to take *Wuthering Heights*, the narration or telling of the story is particularly significant with the complex layering of Lockwood's journal, Nelly Dean's account and various other elements such as letters and reported speech; the time-scheme of the narration itself shifts about further complicating the narrational process.

Not all novels employ such unusual modes of narration, but on the other hand we do tend to become conditioned by the conventions of 'normal' third- or first-person narrators so that we accept any inconsistencies and see any departures from these conventions as unusual. Other theorists have used similar categories to those of Genette; much earlier again the Russian Formalists used *'fabula'* for the story material, and *'suzet'* for the plot: the ways in which the story material is selected, arranged and narrated. These terms have their equivalent as 'histoire' and 'discours' in other modern French narrative theory but are obviously equivalent to the more refined categories of Genette. In British and American narrative criticism a less theorized and structural approach developed in the 1950s and 1960s prior to the advent of European narratology. One of the best examples of this is Wayne C. Booth's *The Rhetoric of Fiction* (1961), in which he emphasizes the importance of seeing a narrative as consisting of a 'teller' and a 'tale', terms he adapts from D.H. Lawrence's maxim: 'Never trust the artist. Trust the tale.' Booth's approach is typical of what might be called Anglo-American empiricism in a pre-theoretical period; it is an extensive, almost exhaustive survey of a wide selection of fictional texts from which he illustrates a range of different kinds of narration, concentrating in particular on the concept of 'point of view'. Reading *The Rhetoric of Fiction* though, highly detailed and scholarly as the book is, it is difficult to derive from it a clear model or terminology through which to address narrative. It is also closer perhaps to a deductive approach rather than the inductive method which Barthes proposed.

Booth's consideration of the term 'point of view' anticipates the term *focalization* as employed by Genette. As Genette shows, the term 'point of view' elides two aspects of narration: the figure who narrates is assumed to be synonymous with the figure in the text from whose perspective the events are seen. However, this is not necessarily so, and indeed the *narrator* and the *focalizer* are usually distinct elements in the narration process. Jane Austen's *Mansfield Park* (1814) is told through a third-person narrator but the focalizer is normally Fanny Price; with third person narration the two are less likely to be confused. In the case of first-person narration, then it does often appear that the narrator and focalizer are one and the same. However, this has to be qualified carefully. In *Great Expectations*, Pip is both narrator and central character, but the language of the narration is that of the adult although the focalizer is more often the child Pip. A passage early in the novel in which Pip describes Mrs Joe reveals this ambivalent mode of narration:

> In the meantime, Mrs Joe put clean white curtains up, and tacked a new flowered-flounce across the wide chimney to replace the old one, and uncovered the little state parlour across the passage, which was never uncovered at any other time, but passed the rest of the year in a cool haze of silver paper, which even extended to the four little white crockery poodles on the mantelshelf, each with a black nose and a basket of flowers in his mouth, and each the counterpart of the other. Mrs Joe was a very clean housekeeper, but had an exquisite art of making her cleanliness more uncomfortable and unacceptable than dirt itself. Cleanliness is next to Godliness, and some people do the same by their religion.[12]

There are more complicated and apparently indistinguishable *narrator/focalizer* relations in texts like Joseph Conrad's *Heart of Darkness* (1899) or Scott Fitzgerald's *The Great Gatsby* (1926), but certainly the two elements can be identified and separated in first-person narrations which are retrospective accounts as in these cases. In *Wuthering Heights*, there is multiple focalization where the role of the focalizer shifts between a range of characters, two of whom are also narrators: Lockwood and Nelly Dean. Recognition of these relations is crucial in analysing narrative method in a text, and also in understanding the consequent privileging of characters and the contingent hierarchies of knowledge and the forms of power expressed through their narrational positions. The apparently combined narrator/focalizer will produce a more coherent, unitary world view than those which are clearly split or multiple, and here we have a significant extension of Bakhtin's view of the novel – which can be extended to other genres – that where there is a plurality of positions which are not obviously unified then we have a more *dialogic* or plural text which does not seek to impose a single world view or ideology. *Wuthering Heights* is interesting in this respect in that the attempt by Lockwood to impose a singular, unified perspective on events is fractured by the focalizers which his narration contains. James Joyce's *Ulysses* foregrounds more explicitly a series of different focalizers who do not impose a rigid hierarchy on the text, but express a more variegated and relative range of views. To turn to poetic texts, in

Browning's 'My Last Duchess' (1842) a significant difference emerges. Although the poem is narrated entirely by the Duke of Ferrara, the narrative allows the reader to construct hypothetical positions or points of focalization outside the narrator's control from which to view the Duke; ironically the alternative focalizers offered are those of his dead wife and the Austrian envoy addressed throughout the poem, who in a sense speak through their silence in encouraging the reader to judge the Duke himself. T.S. Eliot's 'The Love Song of J. Alfred Prufrock' (1917) has a single narrator, but within his psyche arise a plurality of voices or focalizers which question the idea of a unitary personality: 'Let us go then, you and I. ... '

The ideological dimension of narrative has been particularly evident in theories of narrative *closure*. The significance of the ending is clearly paramount in the way that narrative functions; narrative embodies a trajectory which usually comes to some sort of climax or conclusion. By their very form narratives have to finish, but the nature of the ending does vary from a neat conclusion or what E.M. Forster called 'rounding-off' in *Aspects of the Novel*,[13] to more open, unresolved situations. Frank Kermode, in his book *The Sense of an Ending* (1966), explored in a wide-ranging study of texts the ways in which much literature is preoccupied with narratives which work towards visions which embody certain kinds of ending, such as apocalypse or utopia. In this way literary texts could be viewed as being underpinned by larger narratives which circulate across history and culture, a view which had already been strenuously argued in terms of archetypal myths being fundamental to literary works by the Canadian critic Northrop Frye in the 1950s and 1960s. More recently though certain kinds of endings have been seen in much more ideological terms, not so much as reflections of great mythic structures but more as specifically concerned with the social, economic and political relations surrounding a literary text. The term given to this is *closure*, which is usually the ending or point at which the climax or resolution of the narrative is achieved. It has been applied particularly to the nineteenth-century novel, or the *classic-realist* text as several critics and theorists now refer to this genre and its related forms of writing, including much popular fiction, advertising and television serials. The concept of *closure* refers to the ways in which a text persuades a reader to understand and accept a particular 'truth' or form of knowledge, to accept a certain view of the world as valid or natural. *Closure* is not considered to arise directly from the author or to be dependent on the reader's views but to be inherent in a text's form and the writing strategies and reading expectations associated with a particular genre such as the novel. Catherine Belsey defines *closure* in the following terms:

> The moment of closure is the point at which the events of the story become fully intelligible to the reader. The most obvious instance is the detective story where, in the final pages, the murderer is revealed and the motive made plain.[14]

Some theorists such as Belsey have related *closure* to particular kinds or genres of literature, whereas others have argued that it is inherent in all texts but not always at an explicit level, so that works which have apparently 'open', unresolved or ambiguous endings will still contain an ideological closure.

Narrative then is fundamental to literature and a central concern of literary theory. The term can be employed in narrow, and often formalist ways, or in broader and more ideological senses. An understanding of the ways in which narrative functions helps us to make sense of literary texts in ways that more traditional criticism was unable to; it also helps us to interpret other texts and forms of knowledge which circulate in the social world and our relationship to them. Narratives provide both individual and collective ways of seeing, and often work so effectively that we are largely unaware of them as narrative structures. Literary discourse tends to foreground narrative in various ways as we have seen, and perhaps one of literature's most important functions then is to disclose, to reveal, the mechanisms by which meaning is generated, which are more often suppressed in other discourses.

Notes

1 W.J. Courthope, *Liberty and Authority in Matters of Taste* (London, Macmillan, 1896), pp.32–3.
2 Ferdinand de Saussure, *Course in General Linguistics* (London, Fontana, 1978), p. 112. First published in France in 1913.
3 Victor Shklovsky, 'Art as Technique', extracts in Philip Rice and Patricia Waugh, eds., *Modern Literary Theory: A Reader* (London, Edward Arnold, 1989). First published in Russia in 1913.
4 Bertolt Brecht, 'Author's Notes' to *The Life of Galileo* (London, Morhuen, 1963), p. 14.
5 Mikhail Bakhtin, 'Discourse in the Novel', extracts in Philip Rice and Patricia Waugh, eds., *Modern Literary Theory: A Reader* (London, Edward Arnold, 1989). First published in Russia in 1934.
6 Charles Dickens, *Hard Times* (Harmondsworth, Penguin, 1969), p. 65. First published 1854.

7 William Shakespeare, *King Lear* (London, Methuen, 1964), Act III, Sc. iv, ll. 28–36. First performed 1606.

8 George Orwell, *The Road to Wigan Pier* (Harmondsworth, Penguin, 1972), p.17. First published in 1937.

9 The French anthropologist, Claude Lévi-Strauss, demonstrated how cultures share common structures through language and how narratives are embedded in myth. See *Structural Anthropology* (Harmondsworth, Penguin, 1968); first published in France in 1958. Edmund Leach, *Levi-Strauss* (London, Fontana, 1970) is a helpful introduction.

10 Roland Barthes, 'Introduction to the Structural Analysis of Narratives', in *Image-Music-Text* (London, Fontana, 1977), p.79. First published in France in 1966.

11 Fredric Jameson, *The Political Unconscious: Narrative as a Socially Symbolic Act* (London, Methuen, 1981), p.13.

12 Charles Dickens, *Great Expectations* (Harmondsworth, Penguin, 1965), p. 54. First published 1860–61.

13 E.M. Forster, *Aspects of the Novel* (Harmondsworth, Penguin, 1968), p. 170. First published in 1927.

14 Catherine Belsey, *Critical Practice* (London, Methuen, 1980), p. 70.

4 'Society' and the 'individual'

So far the areas which we have looked at have been largely concerned with literature in formal or structural terms and were very much text centred. Such approaches might be accused of ignoring the relationship between literature and what we commonly take to be the 'real world', treating the literary text in isolation and through a rather technical terminology which divorces it from links with people both as individuals and collectively, together with the historical events which compose and surround them. In fact, these theories do help to make much clearer the relationship between literature and what we think of as the real world and also what we take to be history. To start with, they question the common sense view that literature is something *separate from* the world or that it simply *reflects* the world in a passive and mirror-like way. Literature is as much a part and product *of* the world as any other signifying process and is as much a part of reality as a reflection *on* it. It has perhaps been convenient to represent literature as a passive reflection on events rather than as an active event itself, not least because this makes literature a relatively 'safe' commodity, as well as contributing to the myth that literature occupies a kind of ethereal or aesthetically detached position: if anything were intended to separate off literature from material reality then attitudes such as these would seem more effective than those associated with literary theory.

However, literature has traditionally been studied under headings such as 'literature and society', and has been understood as having something important to say about people both individually and collectively. Moreover, a literary text is one of the most vital areas of human 'experience' – to use that problematic term – in the sense of the events represented in the text and the reader's response to them. Whether for theatre audiences or the solitary reading of poetry, literature has occupied a special, privileged position which is not usually accorded to other forms of discourse. Literary theories offer a number of more clearly defined ways of looking at literature than loose formulations such as 'the novel and society'. There is a range of theories which relate to the ways in which literature functions socially and historically, and which help to make explicit the kinds of assumptions which we formulate about literature, and indeed in other forms of discourse which surround us, such as newspapers and those of radio and television. I have chosen to approach these assumptions through the general headings of *Class, Gender, Sexual identity* and *Subjectivity* and to look at some examples of literary theory which have shaped the ways in which we understand these categories. They do overlap considerably: questions of class are bound up with issues of gender and of individual identity, but they do help to clarify what otherwise is in danger of becoming an amorphous and undifferentiated area.

CLASS

In broad terms, society has been composed of various identifiable class groups in different periods of history, these groupings have modified according to historical conditions and also our ability to understand class – the language which describes class has also developed significantly.[1] Literature and literary criticism have had an ambivalent relationship towards issues of class in that much literature and criticism would appear to be oblivious to questions of class, representing the literary work as in some way transcending specific social and historical formations. This is usually because class is either ignored or subordinated to matters concerning the aesthetic properties of a text, or because, according to a traditional humanist approach which could be characterized thus, literature is primarily about *individuals* who represent universal qualities common or potentially common to all men – and presumably women – irrespective of their social and economic position.

Mansfield Park is an example of a text which assumes that the striking economic inequality between some of the characters, most noticeably between Fanny's family and the Bertrams, is quite *natural* and indeed morally acceptable because the main focus of the plot is on the behaviour of individual characters and not on people as members or representatives of economic class groups. Issues of class are only addressed in terms of alignment to a prescribed social hierarchy which manifests itself indirectly, but all the more effectively for this. Perhaps most striking in this respect is the way that the mass of the population in England in the period of the novel is unrepresented in the society of the novel: not even servants or agricultural workers are mentioned. In focusing on a single character as the centre of attention, the text displaces issues of social organization and economic forces in its concentration on individual morality; the heroine Fanny Price appears to be a kind of female Everyman, but in fact comes to represent quite specific class values. Much critical writing on the novel has tended to reinforce this kind of view, concentrating as it does on the fine distinctions of individual morality which Fanny is constantly pre-occupied with and emphasizing the primacy of individuality. Now clearly not all literary works address – or rather fail to address – class in the ways that *Mansfield Park* does, nor does all literary criticism view individual morality as the touchstone of literary quality. But this does provide a convenient example for the ways in which questions of class can be neglected or subordinated, while at the same time partic-ular sets of values which are in fact very much to do with class and the maintenance of the *status quo* can be reinforced precisely by ignoring them. Literary works and literary criticism always have a specific relation to class, and indeed are very much a part of what we call class consciousness, but their orientations to class can vary considerably.

Theories of class originate primarily with Karl Marx in the nine-teenth century, and it is the application and modification of Marxist theory which have been especially influential in ways of thinking about literature historically and socially, as well as culture more generally. It is perhaps worth noting initially that whereas Matthew Arnold saw culture as something which could improve people's lives and was highly desirable to promote and acquire, Marx and his followers saw culture in rather different ways. For Marx, cultural artefacts were related to particular class groups and were considered as being largely designed to reinforce the interests of the controlling or privileged class group, namely the middle class or bourgeoisie, by articulating a view of the world which helped to promote the interests of that class. For example, the 'natural' division of society into unequal economic classes which perform different kinds of work, or the right to the ownership of property by one class in particular we see exemplified in a novel such as *Mansfield Park* and represented more problematically in *Wuthering Heights*. Marx saw class structures as changing over history in a broad sense, so that in feudal times the division of society into the landowners or gentry and peasants or serfs was the result of a different set of economic conditions and consequent system of exploi-tation. Under capitalism a new set of relations obtained between the owners and non-owners of capital. Along with new class formations new cultural forms emerge, and under industrial capitalism the main literary form became the novel: the dominant mode of writing which has already been referred to as classic realism. Marx saw the central historical process of class relations under capitalism as one of *conflict:* that is between the owning or privileged class and the non-owning and exploited class groups. Prior to Marx, the German philosopher Georg Hegel (1770–1831) had argued that the dominant contradiction experienced in life was between the physical or material forces on the one hand and the sense of a spiritual world force or *'Weltgeist'* on the other from which people were alienated but which would eventually be revealed and a state of unity and harmony would follow. Hegel established the concept of *dialectic*, of thesis-antithesis-synthesis which informs Marxist thinking. Marx redefined this contradiction, locating it solely within the material sphere and seeing it manifested in the inequalities experienced by people in their lives, especially in their economic conditions of existence; resolution of this would eventually be brought about by revolution resulting in social change. The spiritual dimension was viewed by Marx as a diversion, as a form of *false consciousness* which distracted people from the real material issues in history. Culture was not for Marx a reflection of some higher spiritual order but rather a product of economic and social forces; this is very clearly put in the famous formulation which reversed conventional assumptions:

> The mode of production of material life conditions the social, political and intellectual life process in general. It is not the consciousness of men that determines their being, but on the contrary, their social being that determines their consciousness.[2]

It is very much around issues of class conflict that writers who have developed Marxist theory, such as Bertolt Brecht, and critics and literary theorists who have also approached literature from a Marxist perspective, have focused their work. Literature, along with other cultural products, is seen primarily as a form of *ideology.*

Ideology

Ideology has become a crucial concept in literary theory, and is taken from Marxist theories of class but can equally be applied to gender, race and other areas which involve the reproduction of unequal relations as *natural* or *normal*. The terms *naturalization* and *normalization* refer to the ways in which we come to think of certain conditions as unquestionably or naturally true, or 'common sense'. In this respect forms of knowledge and ways of representing life, to which literature makes a significant contribution, produce the forms of consciousness which allow people to represent and understand themselves in ways which, according to Marx, are determined by the economic power relations operating in society. A great deal has been written on ideology: at its simplest level it is seen as a way of legitimating the power of the ruling class in society, but this basic model together with the view that ideology is simply a 'superstructural' reflection of the economic base or 'infrastructure' of society has been modified as ideology has been rethought by Marxist theorists. Certainly most theories of ideology see it as creating an illusory or false consciousness which distorts, and even inverts actual historical conditions – rather like photographic plates where the scene taken is turned upside down through the camera's lens. Ideology is generally a provider of comfortable and familiar images too, although it can work in extraordinarily complex ways to achieve its effects, as many advertisements increasingly demonstrate; ideology is not static and works through change and anticipation as well as reinforcing the familiar. Perhaps the most effective ideology is that which we are unaware of, which surrounds us invisibly or which seems to shape itself to our own desires and beliefs without any effort – again to use a simple analogy like a duvet which can assume the contours of our bodies and insulate us effectively in this way.

One of the most important contributions to ideological theory is the essay by the French philosopher Louis Althusser, 'Ideology and Ideological State Apparatuses' (1971). In this essay, Althusser develops the concept of ideology through what he terms *Ideological State Apparatuses* or ISAs in contrast to what he calls *Repressive State Apparatuses* or RSAs. RSAs are ways in which the state controls people directly through established and institutionalized means such as the police, the armed forces, the government administration, the penal system and so on. ISAs are different in that they are not directly or externally imposed forms of ideological coercion but arise from within society. They include areas such as religion, the legal system, education and culture, the media or communications, the various conventions of family life. The difference between RSAs and ISAs is that the latter seem to operate by consensus: that is they appear to be natural and freely chosen, possessing what Althusser calls 'relative autonomy' from the state or the ruling class. In fact, it is argued that as systems of social regulation and control they are far more effective than coercion because people willingly participate in their own subordination and the maintenance of the *status quo*. ISAs are in fact very much bound up with class structure as well as gender and subjectivity. For example, education or the legal system or some forms of culture represent class relations as natural or neutral, implying that in various ways all people are equal, thus disguising or ignoring ways in which people are denied equality through economic or social circumstances. Like Marx, Althusser held that consciousness is constructed through ideologies, but stressed the ways in which ideologies offer systems of meaning and belief which allow people to construct imaginary relations as distinct from the actual relations or conditions in which they live.

To illustrate the idea, we could say that in some forms of literature, for example *Mansfield Park* or *Great Expectations,* class barriers or wealth do not appear as insuperable obstacles to individuals from impoverished classes, and thus allow us to equalize in the imagination what is unequal in social practice. The successful conclusion in *Mansfield Park* for Fanny Price, rising from an impoverished background to a position of high social and economic status, or Pip's gentrification in *Great Expectations* if more ambiguous and qualified, offer the reader myths about individual achievement which bear little relationship to the historical situation of class mobility in the nineteenth century.

Althusser's central thesis is that ideology turns people into *subjects*: that is people are positioned or *interpellated* by forms of communication such as novels to see events in a certain way and to think of themselves as free agents in this process, unified individuals apparently able to read and interpret as they want to but in fact manipulated and restricted by the codes and strategies of the text. By *interpellation,* Althusser means the way in which people are transformed into *subjects,* and are made to assume a particular identity, they are 'recruited' to use one of Althusser's metaphors. The concept of *individualism* is fundamental to western capitalist ideology and inscribed in a wide range of social and cultural discourses; Althusser's contention is that people are not in fact unique and unified individual agents free to determine their own lives but that it is convenient for ruling groups to let people believe they are.

Ideology has continued to develop as a concept, and is itself a contested area in intellectual and theoretical debates. We should not be blind either to what might be called 'the ideology of ideology': that is that Marxist and other discourses lay claims to revealing or unmasking the hidden or illusory aspect of forms of knowledge and culture but may present themselves as neutral or truthful. Marxism for example identifies the 'real' or 'actual' historical conditions as opposed to false ones, and we should thus be aware of Marxist theory itself as a discourse producing certain forms of knowledge, albeit very different from and opposed to, the prevailing discourses of capitalism. In this way ideology can be seen as a more active and challenging practice, not simply reinforcing the familiar and dominant values of society but resisting and counteracting with new and different kinds of knowledge which produce alternative meanings and forms of consciousness. Thus literature cannot be consigned to a purely conservative or reactionary role ideologically. I want to turn now to two developments arising from theories of ideology which apply to literary theory.

Hegemony

The Italian Marxist philosopher Antonio Gramsci, writing in the 1930s, anticipated some of Althusser's theories on ideology; he wrote whilst imprisoned under Mussolini and his works were only published posthumously much later. They have been very influential not least in the area now known as Cultural Studies,[3] which has had a significant impact on redefining both the method and content of traditional English Studies in many academic institutions. Gramsci argued that historically the ruling classes have been able to exercise leadership not through direct coercion but by indirect means; through what he defined as the concept of *hegemony*. Under hegemonic control, people actively work towards their own subordination, which coincides with the continuation of the dominant power groups: as with Althusser's Ideological State Apparatuses, people become unwitting conspirators in their own exploitation and subordination. Gramsci stressed in particular the role of culture as central to hegemony so that a whole range of communications from literature to the mass media, together with activities such as leisure, contribute to this effect of allowing people to 'make sense' of themselves and the world in ways which reinforce and perpetuate the dominant power relations of society. Such forms of knowledge are constantly circulating in society so that people are immersed in ideology in much wider and less explicit ways than more conventional views of ideology allow for.

An important example of this in practice is the kinds of knowledge legitimated and naturalized under the category of 'common sense'. The effectiveness of common sense as a form of knowledge is that its truthfulness appears to require no justification: it seems so because it is so, self-evidently true. It presents itself as obvious, natural, timeless, and yet quite contradictory positions have been rationalized through common sense in different periods of history, from racial persecution and sexual discrimination to corporal punishment and nuclear energy. It should be mentioned though that common sense has also played a more radical role historically, for example in Protestant opposition to the Catholic Church or in Chartists questioning the unequal distribution of wealth: as with most manifestations of ideology, it can be used in quite opposite ways, which in itself undermines the unchallengeability of common sense. If we look at the role of common sense in the nineteenth-century novel, then characters like Joe Gargery in *Great Expectations*, Gabriel Oak in *Far from the Madding Crowd* (1874), or Caleb Garth in *Middlemarch* (1871–2), all of whom can be seen as examples of figures who seem to do what is naturally right according to some innate and unquestionable knowledge, are in fact representative of values which reinforce their social positions and ensure the continuation of a class system based on inequality.

Raymond Williams, in *Marxism and Literature* (1977), sees hegemony as 'a saturation of the whole process of living'; it is distinct from the traditional sense of ideology which tends to view it as something identifiable, in rather narrow and formal terms, which can have a label put on it. Rather it is for Williams:

> a lived system of meanings and values – constitutive and constituting – which as they are experienced as practices appear as reciprocally confirming. It thus constitutes a sense of reality for most people in the society, a sense of absolute because experienced reality beyond which it is very difficult for most members of the society to move, in most areas of their lives. It is, that is to say, in the strongest sense a 'culture', but a culture which has also to be seen as the lived dominance and subordination of particular classes.[4]

Perhaps one reason why the novel in the nineteenth century became so effective as a form of ideology was the range of experience it offered, so that it provided a total immersion effect with a range of discourses circulating which generally tended to complement and support each other, though often involving complex negotiations in order to achieve this; uncomfortable contradictions were thus avoided.

Hegemony though, as with ideology, is a contested site; forms of counter-hegemony can arise and change the dominant values and systems of knowledge. Literature is clearly a potential site for hegemonical debate and struggle, and in a novel such as Robert Tressell's *The Ragged Trousered Philanthropists* (1914) the accepted norms of common sense are challenged and displaced by alternative ways of seeing economic, labour and class relations. In a moment of irony, two of the characters in this novel who represent the capitalist classes in the town of Mugsborough dismiss scientific 'theory' for common sense:

> 'Science is a wonderful thing,' said Mr Sweater at length, wagging his head gravely, 'wonderful!'
> 'Yes: but a lot of it is mere theory, you know,' observed Rushton. 'Take this idear that the world is round, for instance; I fail to see it! And then they say as Hawstralia is on the other side of the globe, underneath our feet. In my opinion it's ridiculous, because if it was true, wot's to prevent the people droppin' orf?'[5]

The novel utilizes quite unconventional techniques, from diagrams to political sermons; in a chapter entitled 'The Oblong', the central character Owen illustrates Marx's theory of surplus value or 'the Money Trick' indicating that in one year 'the workers were robbed of two-thirds of the value of their labour'. The novel works through defamiliarizing techniques, similar to those in Brecht's dramas, where the reader is made to re-examine assumptions and conventions about both social relations and literary form; unlike the nineteenth-century realist novel it does not encourage identification with characters or immersion in the plot. This may help to explain its relatively marginal position in its publishing and academic history until fairly recently.

Discourse

The term *discourse* has been used quite frequently in this book so far, and it could be taken to mean 'language' or 'writing'. However, *discourse* does have particular meanings which are not normally associated with writing or language, it has been employed in anticipation of this section. The term *language* contains assumptions about the world and meaning which could be described as commonsensical; that is, we never really explore or question the relationships between language, meaning and the world because we assume that they just 'are' there. As we have seen in the section on language, it is usually thought that language is a neutral, transparent medium for describing the world and that meaning lies in the world rather than being invested in language itself. The term *discourse* represents a radical and theoretical alternative to these views and locates meaning and our sense or knowledge of the world in language: language is thus the source of our sense of reality and responsible for producing meaning. Now, in a linguistic context this had been implied by Saussure already in the formulation that there can be no *signified* without a *signifier* – that meaning or signification cannot arise without a sign or language to articulate it. But the implications of this in social and ideological terms are much greater. Theories of the 1960s began to suggest that language and social and historical events were inextricably linked, and that particular situations produce certain kinds of language which in turn shape and determine events. Language is produced by a particular set of social relations which obtain at a certain time and place. Such language is never neutral or ideologically innocent, but designed to convey particular kinds of knowledge to achieve certain effects, usually of power and domination.

This view of language as a form of political and social control in which 'truth' becomes more relative and pragmatic rather than absolute and ideal, functioning only in a specific historical context, was promoted most strongly by the French philosopher Michel Foucault. Foucault frequently asserts that we cannot exercise power except through the production of truth:

> 'Western history cannot be dissociated from the way 'truth' is produced and inscribes its effects. We live in a society which to a large extent marches in time with truth – what I mean by that is that ours is a society which produces and circulates discourse with a truth function, discourse which passes for the truth and holds specific powers.'[6]

The social world can be seen as composed of a range of discourses arising and functioning around the institutions which they are part of: in contemporary society for example we can clearly identify the discourses of the legal system, medicine or nuclear physics, though we may not always be aware of the power they exert on our lives. But discourses function in alliance with or in opposition to each other, so that for example in the nineteenth century the general discourses of religion and science appeared to oppose each other in a variety of ways but means of negotiating some sort of compromise or resolution were sought after. In Elizabeth Gaskell's *Wives and Daughters* (1864–6) the plot achieves a resolution between the discourses of tradition in the form of the landed, feudal gentry, and modernity in the form of science and the new rising professional middle classes. The second son of Squire Hamley, Roger, follows a career in science after his elder brother and heir fails miserably at University and secretly marries a French governess; Roger applies his knowledge to the ailing economy of the family estate and also marries Mary Gibson, the daughter of the local medical practitioner. In Chapter 30, 'Old Ways and New Ways', which is a kind of microcosm of the novel's structure and plot, Squire Hamley makes a trip to visit a dying tenant, his former gamekeeper Silas, to discover his rival landowner's agent, Mr Preston, has been trespassing on his land to install modern drainage and Roger Hamley has to restrain him and retrieve the situation. The chapter sets up contrasting discursive fields of medieval squirearchy and feudal loyalties versus modern, aggressive management and agricultural techniques derived from industrial models; the controlling discourse though is that of the fictional narration which works to both counterpoint and then resolve these oppositions through plot and character in ways that achieve a kind of acceptable consensus in the fictional realm.

There are also wider forms of discourse which are not so explicitly or formally institutionalized, but all the more powerful for that perhaps. The discourses of gender and race have operated with modification throughout western history in ways that privilege certain groups and naturalize the inferiorization of others, and they tend to permeate most other discourses. Discourses can interweave with each other, so that within a specific institution employing a certain discourse, other discourses may circulate which inculcate broader social power structures. For example in the discourse of literary criticism it might have been assumed until recently that all readers of literature were male in that the normative reader is usually referred to as 'he', an example of how gender inequalities become naturalized.

Literature itself can be seen as a form of discourse occupying a particular territory, although the position and function of 'English' studies have been considerably redefined in recent years as I have already suggested. Literary discourse has certain distinguishing linguistic characteristics as we have seen, and produces certain kinds of value and 'truth'. Literary texts though can be seen to incorporate many other forms of discourse: indeed literature is perhaps distinctive for being a parasitic form in the way that it borrows from and weaves together very diverse discourses. The nineteenth-century novel again provides a good example of this in the way that strands of economic, scientific, religious, family, moral and other discourses intertwine. Discourses in both social contexts and literary texts are normally arranged or come to organize themselves into some sort of hierarchy where a privileged or controlling discourse exerts power over those which surround it. In the novel this can happen both through the narrative discourse where the narrator's voice exerts authority over the events which it describes, and also via the various institutionalized discourses contained within the narrative; so that in *Mansfield Park* the discourses of property, class, family relations combine to centralize and empower certain figures and values, and to marginalize and eventually exclude others. We might see the typical nineteenth-century novel as a kind of arena for negotiation between different discourses in which acceptable positions are arrived at. Elizabeth Gaskell's *Wives and Daughters* in which the oppositions between religion and natural science together with the emergent middle professional class and the established landed gentry are negotiated and resolved literally and metaphorically through marriage, provides a relatively straightforward example of this process; George Eliot's *Middlemarch* provides a more complex and ambiguous negotiation of similar discursive fields.

By studying a text primarily in terms of its discursive organization instead of the traditional categories such as character, plot and morality, different readings and meanings become available; a new set of textual relations arises in which the historical and ideological operations which take place can be more readily understood. Literary texts can be seen not only as constructions but as important sites of historical debate in which the conflicts and tensions of an age are worked through, either to harmonize and disguise oppositional tendencies, or in an attempt to alter the established and dominant power structures.

Marxist criticism

It would be helpful to introduce some examples of Marxist oriented criticism at this stage, by way of considering some critics who have approached literature from a rather different starting point than those working in a more humanist tradition. Not surprisingly, the main focus initially for such criticism was the novel, and especially the nineteenth-century novel. Marx concentrated his economic and social analysis on this period, and was himself an avid reader of Dickens in particular. The concerns of Marxist critics generally have been primarily social rather than individual, exploring the sociology of the text as opposed to the psychology of individual characters. When characters are examined, it is usually as a way of exploring the wider social and historical forces of which they are seen as products. Significant developments in Marxist literary criticism took place in the 1920s and 1930s and were centred largely on the issue of realism.

The best known and probably most influential critic here is the Hungarian Georg Lukács whose work concentrated mainly on the nineteenth-century novel and questions of *realism*. For Lukács, as with most Marxist critics of his time, a novel must be assessed on its ability to reflect the historical and material conditions of society; these were the main criteria for assessing its realism. Ralph Fox's study, *The*

Novel and the People (1937), is a good example of an English Marxist critic working along similar lines in the same period. Realism was not a question of a text's ability to provide a surface authenticity or versimilitude in terms of detailed physical description but rather to what extent the sense of the underlying historical relations were depicted, how the 'intensive totality' of a work of art relates to the 'extensive totality' of a Marxist vision of history. In fact, Lukács's view of literature is quite idealist even though it might seem to be anti-metaphysical, and he is very much concerned with the way that characters are a part of a total social and historical fabric even though his emphasis might appear to be anti-individual. Lukács and other Marxists rejected the subjective and experimental nature of much modernist writing because such works were too indulgent towards individual consciousness at the expense of a more 'objective' vision, but in a passage where he compares the horse racing scenes in Émile Zola's *Nana* (1880) and Tolstoy's *Anna Karenina* (1874–6), he prefers the latter because the characters are seen from inside and not dehumanized and lifeless. Nevertheless, the resistance by Marxist critics to expressions of and theories on heightened forms of individualism is typified by Ralph Fox:

> Certainly, the modern psychologists have added enormously to the store of our knowledge of man, and the novelist who today neglected their contributions would be as ignorant as he is foolish, but they have failed entirely to see the individual as a whole, as a social individual. They have provided the basis for that false outlook on life which in Proust and Joyce has led to the sole aim of art being, instead of the creation of human personality, the dissociation of human personality.
>
> Psychoanalysis, for all its brilliant and courageous probing into the secret depths of the personality, has never understood that the individual is only a part of the social whole, and that the laws of this whole, decomposed and refracted in the apparatus of the individual psyche like rays of light passing through a prism, change and control the nature of each individual.[7]

Marxist critics have not all been opposed to experimentation though; at the point of the Russian revolution prior to the return to more traditional theories of realism in Russia, radical theorists such as Victor Shklovsky had argued that art needs to shock, to *defamiliarize* and subvert our sense of the normal, as we have already seen. Two Marxist writers of the 1930s developed theoretical, critical and creative practices which offer a very different approach to literature from that typified by Lukács. As I have argued above, the dramatist Bertolt

Brecht introduced the concept of defamiliarization by breaking with the conventions of theatrical realism. Rather than striving to create an illusion of reality on stage, he revealed the mechanisms by which such illusions are created so that the audience was encouraged to reflect critically on the action presented and think about the ways in which it was constructed, considering possible alternatives to it – his term for this technique was *verfremdungseffekte* or 'alienation effect'. The implications of Brecht's works are that if drama is revealed as constructed rather than providing an illusory 'reality', and if drama is a reflection on society, then society too is open to change as it also is perceived as constructed. Literature, rather than being a passive reflector, reinforcing established values and norms of society, can become an active agent or catalyst for social change. Whereas Lukács saw a kind of integrated or organic totality in his view of realism, Brecht's 'epic' theatre was constructed around fragmentation and discontinuity; by classic standards of formal unity derived from Aristotle it could be judged as bad drama aesthetically, but that was the very point. Brecht showed that aesthetics and ideology are inextricably linked, and that to change the prevailing ideology the dominant aesthetic has to be fractured and reconstructed.

Along with Brecht's dramatic theory and practice, the work of the German critic Walter Benjamin is very significant. Benjamin argued in his essay 'The Work of Art in the Age of Mechanical Reproduction' (1933) that the technological revolution which was taking place in the early twentieth century in terms of the media and mass circulation of texts of all kinds was potentially a liberating force for people who had hitherto been denied access to artistic production: everybody was now potentially an artist because the means of expression were becoming available. Art for Benjamin was not so much a question of individual talent but the material problem of gaining access to means of communication. Further to this, the new media of film and photography could break down the traditional conception of art as something remote and inaccessible: not only was the camera more easily available but film allows for new representations of reality, for rapid change and movement which can express the fragmentation and discontinuity which Brecht was striving for in his dramatic productions. In a slightly later essay, 'The Author as Producer' (1934), Benjamin saw the artist not as someone producing a detached reflection of reality but as being directly engaged with and integral to reality. The classical notion of art as a mirror held up to life was shattered.

Another group of Marxist critics and philosophers, known collectively as the Frankfurt School, strongly opposed Benjamin's ideas about the mass circulation of art. The main figures were Theodor Adorno, Max Horkheimer and Herbert Marcuse who formed the Institute of Social Research at Frankfurt. This was exiled from Germany in 1933, re-formed in America and returned to Germany in 1950. Their position is different from that of Lukács, and from Brecht and Benjamin. They dismissed realism as reinforcing conventional ways of thinking, together with popular forms of culture which they saw as stultifying – ironically here they had something in common with F.R. Leavis though at opposite ends of the political spectrum. The kind of literature they celebrated was that which expressed a detachment from reality, and much modernist experimental work was seen as offering insights which more conventional writing could not. Adorno's conception of art in particular is quite elitist in that he stresses the need to go beyond what is palatable to the masses who will reject anything experimental because it disturbs their vision.

As we can see from these fairly early Marxist approaches, any suggestion that Marxist theory and criticism are a homogeneous body of ideas would be very mistaken. This is all the more so in Marxist work from the 1960s onwards, with the institutionalization of the large theoretical movement known as structuralism, and the movements which have followed, known usually as poststructuralism and deconstruction. Structuralist theories generally see language or signifying systems as the fundamental matter of human existence, whereas for traditional Marxists it is history and the material conditions of existence which exist outside of language (see Chapter 5 under 'Structuralism' and 'Poststructuralism'). Various attempts have been made to synthesize these apparently incompatible approaches, and reassess the role of literature as a consequence. The Romanian theorist Lucien Goldmann in *The Hidden God* (1964) has argued that more than any other kind of activity, literature is capable of expressing what he termed a 'world vision', that is 'the whole complex of ideas, aspirations and feelings which links together the members of a social group (a group which, in most cases, assumes the existence of a social class) and which opposes them to members of other social groups.'[8] Unlike most structuralist approaches, Goldmann sees the necessity of locating literary texts in the historical period in which they are produced, but unlike most Marxists also identifies underlying structural relationships between quite disparate areas: literature, social history and religion.

Two more French Marxist theorists and critics, Louis Althusser, whom we have already looked at under ideology, and Pierre Macherey have also developed arguments on the role of literature which endow it with a special status. Althusser views literature generally as performing a rather ambiguous function in that it both acts as a form of ideology, thus blinding people to their real conditions of existence, but also is capable of detaching itself from the very ideology in which it participates, thus drawing attention to the imaginary relations which it describes. Effectively Althusser is saying that some literature reinforces the dominant values, some questions them, and some does both. Macherey arrives at a similarly ambiguous position in his book *A Theory of Literary Production* (1966) but through a rather different approach. He argues that a text functions at two levels: that of the surface ideology where we are conscious of the natural, obvious relations between events; and a hidden or unconscious level where the flaws of the surface are exposed, where we perceive fractures in the supposed unity of the text. These unconscious moments may be in the form of silences or absences, things which are not allowed to enter into the dominant ideological discourse, or take the form of contradictions and inconsistencies. To take the example of *Mansfield Park* again, there is a contradiction in the text which is glossed over regarding Fanny Price's innate moral goodness and her natural relationship to the country gentry represented by her feelings for the house Mansfield Park, but her character is not explained by her upbringing in the chaotic and deprived household of her family at Portsmouth.

Two critics who perhaps have contributed most to recent Marxist theory are, in Britain, Terry Eagleton and, in America, Fredric Jameson. Both have developed – and indeed continued to modify – distinctive conceptions of literary studies. Eagleton has insisted on the need for a theorized approach to literature and indeed at one stage attacked Raymond Williams, his former teacher who owes much to Marxist theory, for being too empirical in his work. Eagleton's own position is again rather different from that of Althusser, and other Marxists who have allowed literature a special role, although there would appear to be some exceptions in his views on writers such as Blake or Brecht. Ideology becomes for him a much more complex area than some Marxists have allowed for, seeing literature as a complex reworking and reinscribing of ideology. In an essay on Conrad's *The Secret Agent* (1907)[9] for example, a text which has been seen as a radical critique of capitalism, Eagleton views the novel as ultimately reinforcing the *status quo* through its complex strategies. Eagleton also links the discourse of literary criticism to the study of literature more explicitly than previously had been done, and argues for a re-conception of literature by changing the ways in which literature is constructed as a body of culture and knowledge. He has opposed the French inspired but now heavily American-based school of 'deconstruction', discussed in the next chapter, arguing that it negates any firm sense of reality or knowledge, which for a Marxist is difficult if not impossible to accept.

Fredric Jameson views Marxism as the only antidote to the advance of western monopoly capitalism. As with Eagleton, he stresses the role of criticism in his study of major twentieth-century Marxist critical thought, *Marxism and Form* (1971), and calls for what he terms a 'dialectical criticism'. Jameson states that 'our judgements on the individual work of art are ultimately social and historical in character', and views literature as part of a larger and constantly changing historical process which is dependent primarily on the critic's or reader's situation; the historical context of reading becomes the site of the production of meaning rather than the context in which a work was written which is a secondary context reconstructed by the critic. In a later work, *The Political Unconscious: Narrative as Socially Symbolic Act* (1981), Jameson develops an approach similar to that of Macherey in which literature works as a form of ideological discourse which represses historical truth, but which, as in Freudian analysis, can be reached through the gaps, slips and silences which betray the repression. Jameson acknowledges that all literary criticism or interpretive strategies are themselves inherently ideological: that is they construct forms of 'truth' and writers, including critics, cannot avoid colluding with this process. Jameson's answer is that we need to be aware of the ideology of ideology insofar as this is possible: such self-consciousness is preferable to those discourses which do not draw attention to their own truth-producing mechanisms.

This is a bare sketch of Marxist criticism, but it should be apparent that it is an important area of theoretical work and a significant contrast to other kinds of theoretical and critical approaches. It may well be more helpful to think of Marxist theory not so much in terms of its individual practitioners as I have done above, but more as an ongoing body of knowledge or discourse with its own narrative pattern, conflicts and contradictions, but based upon certain fundamental precepts about the nature of society and history.

GENDER

This section is mainly concerned with developments in feminist criticism and critical theory, and with approaches to writing which have drawn attention to issues of gender and the place of women in literature. The reason for this is that in western society and culture the male is regarded as the norm, as the central and neutral position from which the female is a departure. Simone de Beauvoir expresses it thus in *The Second Sex* (1949):

> Thus humanity is male and man defines woman not in herself but as relative to him; she is not regarded as an autonomous being .... She is defined and differentiated with reference to men and not he with reference to her; she is the inessential as opposed to the essential. He is the Subject, he is the Absolute – She is the Other.[10]

This is no more evident than in language, literary and non-literary. In most discourses the positions of power are explicitly acknowledged to be male, for example 'chairman'; or, where we are talking about people generally, as with the 'reader' in literary criticism, then these positions are implicitly assumed to be male in character.

As with the class system, gender differences are socially constructed though usually presented as natural or normal. There is an important distinction to be made between *sex* and *gender. Sex* is a term which can be used to indicate the biological differences between men and women, but *gender* signifies the socially constructed differences which operate in most societies and which lead to forms of inequality, oppression and exploitation between the sexes. Both *femininity* and *masculinity* are socially constructed and invested with various qualities, values, images and narratives which constantly circulate in society and which shape and determine people's attitudes and lives. Advertising is a good example of these processes at work, and John Berger's *Ways of Seeing* (1972) analyses the ways in which advertising as well as oil painting utilizes gender positions of male power and female subservience. Clearly literature as a major form of communication plays a very significant role in this area, along with the discourse of literary criticism – and indeed those of literary and critical theory; they can work as both agents of reinforcement and of subversion in the ways that they construct or represent gender relations.

As with the previous section, this can be no more than a brief introduction to the background and some of the key issues and theories associated with women's writing and feminist criticism, but the suggested further reading does point to a range of critical and theoretical material from introductory to more complex works which interested readers may wish to pursue. For a more detailed introduction to this topic, Pam Morris's book *Literature and Feminism* (1993), is very helpful.

Women and literature

A number of issues regarding the representation of women in literature began to be addressed in the twentieth century, mainly by women writers such as Virginia Woolf and then by feminist literary critics. This is not to say that there were not earlier attempts to call into question the position of women through a literary medium: Mary Wollstonecraft's *A Vindication of the Rights of Woman* (1792) argued for the need to improve women's education, and nineteenth-century novelists such as George Eliot in Britain and George Sand in France attacked established social attitudes to women, albeit not so radically as some of their twentieth-century successors. The main issue which has become increasingly significant is, to what extent are the experiences and voices of women represented in literature? There are several further issues related to this. Can a male writer adequately represent women characters and female experience? On the other hand, if language generally and the institution of literature are male dominated, then can a woman writer break out of these restrictions to articulate a genuinely female consciousness? This latter point too has been contested by some feminist critics who argue that to identify a specific form of 'female experience', as for example Elaine Showalter has in *A Literature of Their Own* (1977), is to work counterproductively in reinforcing the myth that all women have similar forms of experience.

Historically, as with class and race, literature has arguably tended to subordinate or marginalize the position of women. This has happened in several ways. In literary texts, women usually play less significant roles than men; obviously there are exceptions in works by both male and female writers, but the dominant or normative experience represented in literature is, it has been argued by feminists from Virginia Woolf onwards, male. It is not only a question of characters, but also of the kind of subjects which are deemed worthy of treatment: until relatively recently there have been very few if any literary works which deal with the trials and tribulations of child bearing and rearing, something which is central to the experience of a large proportion of the populations of countries which possess a literary culture. Then in the cultural institution of literature as studied on academic syllabuses and the selection of works which form the 'canon', male writers and the male point of view have been privileged. Feminist critics have argued that the canon is a reflection of the dominant power group in society, that is male as well as middle- or upper-class and white. Those texts by women which are included tend to be as 'honorary men', conforming to male views of reality or reinforcing male views of women in presenting stereotypical female characters and experience. Recent attempts have been made to redress this imbalance in the institutionalized apparatuses of literature, so that some publishing houses will only publish books written by women, and increasingly literary studies involve courses on women's writing or feminist criticism – and not only as options. Dale Spender, in *Mothers of the Novel* (1986) has shown that another tradition can be identified consisting of women novelists in contrast to the predominantly male-dominated tradition typified by Ian Watt's account of *The Rise of the Novel* (1957).

Literary criticism is the other area which has been questioned by feminist theory in that most criticism assumed values and adopted criteria which again centralized male views and experience and marginalized those of women. Even if a women student was reading a novel by a woman about women characters, the mode of critical approach would be normalized from a male perspective. The American feminist critic Annette Kolodny has demonstrated how education and the critical process position and condition readers to see and 'appreciate' texts in certain permissible ways. She argues that reading is a form of engagement not with texts, but with *paradigms*: that is, 'we appropriate meaning from a text according to what we need (or desire), or in other words, according to the critical assumptions or predispositions (conscious or not) that we bring to it.'[11] Reading is a socialized, or learned activity, and our reading habits can become fixed around the normative, and therefore male, assumptions and conventions of society. She cites her own experience of reading and taking pleasure in Milton's *Paradise Lost* (1667), which, as both a Jew and a feminist, she found contradictory as she could not 'subscribe to its theology, nor to its hierarchy of sexual valuation.' Her explanation is that she had acquired and learnt to manipulate certain critical strategies – an 'interpretative model' – which positioned her in such a way as to appreciate the poem, but from the perspective of a particular set of gender and theological conventions which were not her own; in 'learning to read the text properly', any resistant or oppositional interpretations had been effectively cancelled out, as had her individual identity.

Feminist theory and criticism

Virginia Woolf's *A Room of One's Own* (1928), although not a theoretical work in the conventional sense of the term, does serve as a point of departure for the study of women's literature and the beginnings of a feminist criticism. On this point, it is worth noting that some feminist critics have avoided the discourse of literary theory as a further extension of male discourse and hence domination in literary studies, and certainly the power and perhaps the linguistic properties of much theoretical writing do make this a valid position. Leading on from this, it would be dangerous to characterize feminist theory as a unified discourse: by its nature most feminist writing tries to eschew a singular, centralized vision for a more plural and decentred range of approaches. It would be more appropriate in this context to talk of *feminisms*.

Virginia Woolf was also part of a larger movement of women writers who had adopted a specifically female point of view in the early twentieth century such as Katherine Mansfield, Rebecca West and Dorothy Richardson. As with Marxism, it is dangerous to characterize feminist writing in terms of individual personalities, and it is helpful to see Virginia Woolf's writing as part of a larger movement or new discourse which began to challenge the dominant discourses of gender; it is also an attempt to recover and explore points made by other women writers which had hitherto been largely ignored. Virginia Woolf's main argument regarding the lack of women writers is the material conditions which women live under, having little or no financial independence and generally expected to serve the needs of men. It was not that women were unable to write: she demonstrates this with the example of Aphra Behn who was forced to write to survive after the death of her husband, and then discusses the increasing numbers of women writers in the eighteenth and nineteenth centuries. But most of these women were writing not as a profession, but more often as a diversion: the institutions of literature were still essentially male controlled, as was domestic life. Woolf takes the hypothetical example of Shakespeare's sister, suggesting that had she existed and possessed the same qualities of genius as Shakespeare the man, then they would never have been allowed to come to fruition and express themselves on paper because she would have been forced to assume the roles imposed on women of domestic work and motherhood. She agrees with a bishop who is supposed to have said that it would be impossible for a woman to have the genius of Shakespeare, not because women could not possess these qualities but because they would not be able to express them in such a male-dominated society.

One of Virginia Woolf's most significant contributions to feminist criticism is the discussion on language which anticipates more recent work. It is a rather untheorized approach to language in that she talks of the 'male' and 'female' sentence without analysing their respective characteristics beyond an impressionistic level, but she identifies the ideological role of language in constructing gender. This has been subsequently developed and theorized by feminist critics such as Dale Spender in *Man Made Language* (1980):

> The semantic rule which has been responsible for the manifestation of sexism in the language can be simply stated: there are two fundamental categories, *male* and *minus male*. To be linked with male is to be linked to a range of meanings which are positive and good: to be linked to minus male is to be linked to the absence of those qualities.... The semantic structure of the English language reveals a great deal about what it means to be female in a patriarchal order[12]

Language, as we have seen, is constitutive of knowledge as discourse, and it is possible to see the privileging of the male position and the establishment of a patriarchal order in broader historical and discursive ways as well as in everyday or literary language. In *Invisible Women* (1982), Dale Spender argues that knowledge does not exist independently from people, 'waiting for brilliant men to discover it and to make impartial records uncoloured by their own opinions and beliefs', but that it is constructed 'in accordance with the values and beliefs with which they begin.'[13] Thus philosophy, science, indeed all forms of knowledge which are produced from a predominantly male perspective in a language which itself reinforces such a viewpoint, will be male centred and discriminate against women. In terms of power, Spender argues it is not in the interests of the dominant group to challenge the basis of the oppression of groups which are characterized as inferior and incompetent.

Literary criticism, as one kind of discourse and as a form of knowledge, has reinforced patriarchal order in various ways. The construction of a male-dominated canon is one feature of this as we have seen, but there are other aspects which have been challenged or problematized by feminist approaches. The myth of literature as an accurate representation of reality which derived from the idea of mimesis central to the humanist criticism preceding any theoretical approaches, and which is still powerful, has become an area of debate in feminist theory. The nineteenth-century novel is a form which employs techniques of classic realism, and which women writers such as Charlotte Brontë or George Eliot used to write about women. But what this view of literature does not take into account, as argued by Cora Kaplan in *Sea Changes: Culture and Feminism* (1986), is that literary texts are constructed from within ideology and the 'reality' they articulate is dependent on the historical culture which surrounds them; so too are the literary critical claims about their truthfulness or authenticity determined by the culture from which they arise. Kaplan links gender to class and subjectivity, and suggests that women writers, in appropriating the literary discourse of realism to provide an apparently realistic representation of women, and feminist criticism in celebrating these writers, whilst challenging the patriarchal order generally, is also colluding in denying the representation of women outside the limits of realism:

> It is hard for feminism to accept the implications of this virtual refusal of textual realism, if only because literature was one of the few public discourses in which women were allowed to speak for themselves, where they were not the imaginary representations of men. None the less, the subjectivity of women of other classes and races and with different sexual orientations can never be 'objectively' or 'authentically' represented in literary texts by the white, heterosexual, middle-class woman writer, however sympathetically she invents or describes such women in her narrative.[14]

This kind of debate within feminist approaches should not be seen as a weakening of the feminist position; indeed, as Toril Moi has pointed out in *Sexual/Textual Politics: Feminist Literary Theory* (1985), to pretend that feminist theory is a univocal body of knowledge would be inaccurate and detrimental to feminism. Nevertheless, Toril Moi does identify two intellectual traditions in feminist theory: Anglo-American and French. The former Moi sees as being more concerned with developing a political position as a challenge to the forms of male domination in the institutions of literature and literary study: in particular the literary canon. Feminist theorists and critics such as Elaine Showalter and Ellen Moers have done much to establish an alternative tradition of women writers, recovering works by novelists such as Charlotte Perkins Gilman or Kate Chopin, but Moi argues they have displaced one canon by another without challenging the idea of hierarchy and the authority of the text conceived as a way of transmitting universal human experience: 'The feminist reader is not given leave to get up and challenge this female voice; the Female Text rules as despotically as the old male text.'[15] Although Moi recognizes the radical nature of Anglo-American feminist literary criticism and theory as a political enterprise, she also sees it as trapped within conventional humanist approaches to the text whereby the author–reader relationship remains unchallenged and the authentic 'experience' contained in the text is used to validate a certain view of women which passes as universal.

By contrast, Moi turns to the French feminist tradition which is characterized by more attention to the text itself and a strong interest in psychoanalytical theory, and which does not necessarily see women writers producing a female voice, or entirely exclude male writing. French theory generally draws on a more diverse range of influences, and does not adopt such explicitly centralized positions as some Anglo-American feminists have: one of the criticisms made against Julia Kristeva or Hélène Cixous is that they produce contradictory or anarchic positions in their writing. But to move beyond the positions offered by conventional (male) discourse for both writing and reading, it may well be that an initial unintelligibility will be a feature of their language, as opposed to a readily intelligible if radical discourse of the Anglo-American tradition. The stress on the text by French feminists is also very much an emphasis on *writing*, on the productive pleasures of writing and reading which can lead to emphasizing the varied and multiple forms of subjectivity that are not encouraged in the Anglo-American approach. In this way, patriarchal discourse is undermined through *play* rather than by confrontation or exclusion. Following the French approach, there is in a sense no need for a canon, or for the various categories of literature which have been so much the hallmark of western culture and 'English' studies.

SEXUAL IDENTITY

Gender and sexual forms of differentiation have been theorized in ways that partly develop, but which also depart from feminist theories. The view that sexual identity is a function of social convention and conditioning is not a recent phenomenon though; Virginia Woolf's experimental novel *Orlando* (1928), in which the eponymous central character undergoes a sex change, makes the point that an individual's identity need not be determined by sex or gender:

> Orlando had become a woman – there is no denying it. But in every other respect, Orlando remained precisely as he had been. The change of sex, though it had altered their future, did nothing whatever to alter their identity. Their faces remained, as their portraits prove, practically the same. His memory – but in future we must, for convention's sake, say 'her' for 'his' and 'she' for 'he' – her memory then, went back through all the events of her life without encountering any obstacle. Some slight haziness there may have been, as if a few dark drops had fallen into the clear pool of memory; certain

things had become a little dimmed; but that was all. The change seemed to have been accomplished painlessly and completed in such a way that Orlando herself showed no surprise at it.[16]

Oscar Wilde's dramas transgress to some extent the behaviour of stereotypical gendered roles, for example through the creation of strong female and weak male characters, although paradoxically these inversions do not seem to pose a threat to established conventions to judge by their reception history. Radclyffe Hall's *The Well of Loneliness* (1928) also explores explicitly sexual ambivalence and inversion in the character of Stephen Gordon whose female sex cannot be accepted by her aristocratic parents desiring a male heir, and whose androgynous characteristics defy social convention. Unlike the playfulness of Virginia Woolf's trans-historical character Orlando though, Stephen is caught up in historical circumstances and cannot see sex and gender as a trivial pursuit. Sexual identity has become an increasingly significant theme in literary texts in recent years, for example in Jeanette Winterson's fiction, from her first novel *Oranges Are Not The Only Fruit* (1985) which explores the central character's discovery and celebration of lesbian relationships, to *The Passion* (1987) and *Sexing the Cherry* (1989) which both merge female and male characteristics and involve ungendered narratives of love. Manuel Puig's novel *The Kiss of the Spiderwoman* (1979) and Hector Babenco's film version (1985) question the conventions of sexual and gender identity, and several recent films have employed these themes centrally in their narratives such as Neil Jordan's *The Crying Game* (1992) or John Waters' *Hairspray* (1988) with Divine; it is interesting that both *The Kiss of the Spiderwoman* and *The Crying Game* utilize transgender themes to transcend violent and oppressive political regimes as well as social convention.

The problematics of gender and sexual identity have been increasingly theorized. Judith Butler's *Gender Trouble: Feminism and the Subversion of Identity* (1990) questions the 'binary relation between "men" and "women", and the internal stability of those terms.' She argues that 'female' is no longer a stable term, and that one problem with feminist theory is that it can reinforce the very power structures it seeks to question by its relational insistence: by setting itself constantly in relation to the male subject it seeks to depart from. She also questions Foucault's methodology in its 'genealogical critique' which 'refuses to search for the origins of gender, the inner truth of female desire, a genuine or authentic sexual identity that repression has kept from view'. Foucault, she argues, mistakes the effects of institutions and discursive practices as origins and causes, and her project is 'to center on – and decenter – such defining institutions: phallogocentrism and compulsory heterosexuality.'[17]   Gender 'indeterminacy' as she calls it, may not imply the failure of feminism, but rather begin to establish the fundamental issue of identity in its primary forms. Marjorie Garber, in *Vested Interests: Cross-Dressing and Cultural Anxiety* (1992) considers transvestism and its manifestation through cross-dressing to be an expression of resistance to gender categorization and regulation from medieval and Renaissance Europe to the present day: 'transvestism was the spectre that rose up – both in the theatre and the streets – to mark and overdetermine the crisis of social and economic change.'[18] For Garber, 'one of the most important aspects of cross-dressing is the way in which it offers a challenge to easy notions of binarity, putting into question the categories of "female" and "male", whether they are considered essential or constructed, biological or cultural.'[19]

Lesbian and more recently gay theories have played an increasingly significant role in literary and cultural studies. Diana Fuss in *Inside/Out: Lesbian Theories, Gay Theories* (1991) also questions the binary opposition of hetero/homosexual structures, what she calls the 'inside' and 'outside' and argues for the need for 'interrogating the position of "outsiderness" where much recent lesbian and gay theory begins, implicitly if not always directly raising the questions of the complicated processes by which borders are constructed, sexual identities assigned, and sexual politics formulated.'[20] Jonathan Dollimore in *Sexual Dissidence: Augustine to Wilde, Freud to Foucault* (1991) argues that the gendered opposition of the 'dominant and the subordinate' and the resistance to such heterosexual orthodoxy, which he terms 'sexual dissidence' whose 'literature, histories, and subcultures ... though largely absent from current debates (literary, psychoanalytic, and cultural), prove remarkably illuminating for them.'[21] Sexual deviation, he argues, has been associated with artistic inadequacy and, developing Foucault's ideas, also deviation from the truth. In a wide-ranging study of literary texts, history and theories Dollimore demonstrates how paradoxically significant homosexual themes are culturally in spite of the marginalization, denunciation and persecution of homosexuals throughout history.

SUBJECTIVITY

The emphasis of this chapter so far has been more concerned with people as groups; Marxism as a philosophy stresses the primacy of class over individuality in society, and most of the feminist approaches have been interested in the experience of women collectively. Yet usually our first encounter with literature is very much what we think of as an individual experience. We read usually alone: the physical act of reading is a solitary pastime, and most literary texts articulate what seems to be highly individual experience, whether it be in a Shakespearian sonnet or a nineteenth-century novel. Most texts contain individualized characters with whom we tend to identify as readers, though clearly some readers will identify more or less strongly with different characters. Literature as a discourse seems to confirm our sense of individuality, indeed our uniqueness and independence in the world from those around us. And at the same time it also gives us the sense that we can identify with another person or persons: that characters have similar experiences to us and *vice versa*. The humanist tradition or ideology lays particular emphasis on the individual, especially from the Renaissance period onwards; at certain points in literary history the individual has acquired remarkable transcendent qualities in writing as different as the Romantic poetry of Coleridge or adventure stories by John Buchan.

Humanist views place 'man' at the centre of the universe and see the individual as the source and end of ideas, action and meaning; the world is explained primarily in individualized terms. Philosophy and literature in this tradition have tended to stress the uniqueness and autonomy of each individual, emphasizing freedom of choice, the imagination and the power of individual action. The narratives of history generally reinforce this, concentrating frequently on exceptional individuals rather than on collective groups, and the rise of biography and autobiography especially in the nineteenth century offered a further extension of and concentration on the individual. Works which questioned the individual and sought to relegate such figures or abolish the hero, for example Émile Zola's *Germinal* (1885) or Tressell's *The Ragged Trousered Philanthropists*, are very much exceptions and are not usually considered as 'great' works of literature partly because they fail to present reality in terms of the fully rendered consciousnesses of individuals. At the same time as possessing unique qualities, individuals were seen as sharing a common essence or core, some basic kind of touchstone represented in various ways: as a soul, as basic common decency, as common sense, and so on; this could transcend the differences of individuality which allowed for a cohesive fabric to connect people together in their individuality. This quality though was still located in the individual, and not in more social or collective forms of knowledge or organization.

A number of theories which are sometimes placed under the general term *poststructuralism*, more to place them historically rather than for any homogeneity in outlook, have questioned the status of the individual. To begin with, they replace 'individual' with the term *subject* in order to draw attention to a different approach and understanding to the concept, in the same way that *discourse* has displaced 'language' or *closure* has been introduced to rethink ending or resolution. By *subject*, two meanings are indicated. First there is the idea of the grammatical subject, that is the sense of individuality which language allows us so that we can say 'I' and differentiate ourselves from those other members of society who surround us. Allied to this is the broader sense of the individual subject as conceived in humanist and idealist philosophy: that is the individual mind as the site of consciousness and meaning as distinct from the world around it. The other and very different meaning is the individual in a political sense, as the subject of law or subject of the political state. This suggests that the individual is not free to determine his or her life, but *subject* to the forces of control which operate in a given society. What this approach does is to dismantle or *deconstruct* the processes by which the individual has been traditionally thought of or constructed as the centre of the world and reality. Rather than possessing individual freedom and a unique, unified consciousness, people as subjects were now viewed as socially constructed through language, or discourse, and the various institutions and forms of communication which circulated and reinforced the sense of individual identity. Further, the individual was no longer considered a coherent, unified, self-contained entity, but became fragmented and a site of conflict in that various forces were seen to position and construct him/her in different and often contradictory ways.

Subjectivity and character

The site of subjectivity in literary texts is normally centred on the device of *character*. This seems obvious and automatic because we have become so conditioned to character as a textual device for constructing ways of seeing and explaining events, and indeed that is the reason why character is so *natural* and powerful as a device or strategy in literary texts. *Character* is the figure in literary discourse which equates with our sense of individuality in other discourses; the first point of recognition, of 'familiarity' in a text, is the way in which we assemble a sense of character. As Louis Althusser has stated, obviousness is a very powerful way of making people accept things as real or natural:

Obviousness ... is the elementary ideological effect. ... Like all obvious-
nesses, including those that make a word 'name a thing' or 'have a meaning'
(therefore including the obviousness of the 'transparency of language'), the
'obviousness' that you and I are subjects – and that does not cause any
problems – is an ideological effect, the elementary ideological effect.[22]

Much early literary criticism colluded in this obviousness in that
literary texts were seen primarily as being about people who, though
often thought of as fictional, still led lives equivalent to our own and
were assessed in terms of their lifelike qualities and consistency.
Character study dominated criticism, indeed it arguably still does in
many institutions where exam papers frequently have character-
centred questions and the initial approach to a work is usually, and
sometimes uncritically, through character as the most obvious or
natural point of access. Prior to the advent of recent European literary
theory in Britain, the critic L.C. Knights had pointed out the fallacy of
treating characters as if they were equivalent to real people in an essay
called 'How Many Children Had Lady Macbeth?' (1933) and more
generally attacked the prevalent preoccupation of literary critics with
character to the exclusion of what he termed the more 'poetic' features
of a text. Certainly the approaches of these critics help to confirm the
thesis by Lukács and others regarding the ideological nature of literature, especially the novel, which is culturally central to the
development of our sense of subjectivity and reinforced as such by
character-centred interpretations.

Literary and critical theory, and more generally theories of ideology, have resulted in a very different view of character in literary texts.
In social terms, individual subjectivity is explained by Althusser and a
number of theorists as being constructed through language and other
social processes. Literature, through a range of devices, produces a
sense of subjectivity both in the reader whose sense of his or her own
subjectivity is confirmed by the text, and at a secondary level in the
literary text itself through the construction of further imaginary subjects or characters. The essential subject in the reading process is the
reader, and normally the reader is addressed in such a way that the text
coheres around him or her; devices such as point of view and narration
allow events to be seen and interpreted in specific ways. There are of
course texts which subvert the reader's position as a subject – good
examples are Italo Calvino's *If on a Winter's Night a Traveller* or much
earlier Lawrence Sterne's *Tristram Shandy*, but these are exceptions
from the norm. The process of the reader 'making sense' of a text
further privileges his or her subject position, as does identification with

a central character or narrator. Tolstoy's strategy in *Anna Karenina* is to manipulate the reader to experience vicariously events from Levin's point of view; the reader is positioned so that Levin's individual, and often intensely subjective, observations and insights come to form the dominant, natural way of interpreting the events represented in the text. Where alternative positions are offered, then these are expressed through the subjective experiences of individual characters. As Robin Wood points out in an essay on *Anna Karenina*, 'Levin and the Jam' (1979), Tolstoy pushes realism to its limits in the rendering of individualized experience: Levin's character is psychologically plausible and coherent, 'Yet this is the essence of "Realist" strategy: to impose a general ideology through the psychological plausibility of a particular case.'[23] Althusser, as we have seen, calls the process of recognition and identification *interpellation* whereby individuals are 'hailed' or addressed in ways which position them. The reader is drawn towards Levin and becomes through him the experiencing centre of the novel's organic vision; unless we resist such positioning by reading against the grain, it is hard to avoid the process. This is especially the case in classic realist literature where we are invited as readers to share the insights of central characters or the narrator so that the sense we make of the text as reading subjects is mirrored in the way that characters and/or narrators make sense out of the events they 'experience'. As Pip begins increasingly to understand his situation and reaches certain moral insights in *Great Expectations*, or as Fanny makes certain decisions which are confirmed by the narrator in *Mansfield Park*, so the reader feels that he/she is arriving at an understanding but seemingly doing so independently. In fact, the strategies of the text usually ensure that such an understanding is unavoidable unless we deliberately read against the grain. The reader is thus placed in a privileged position, one of *dominant specularity* to use theoretical terminology, through being offered a subject position which allows him/her to assess and judge characters and events in the novel. This provides the illusion of independent thought and reinforces the myths of individuality and the power attached to them which circulate outside the literary text. Most literary texts, whether poetry, drama or fiction, offer a subject position which is often in the form of a character from which to view the action or experience narrated, and this position is hard to resist.

The emphasis of much literary theory has been to examine texts in ways which do not always begin with or prioritize character-centred approaches; or, where character is discussed, to be aware of this as a textual device and part of the conventions of literary discourse generally. The fascination of character in a liberal-humanist tradition of writing and criticism, wherein the key issues were concerned with an individual's real nature or identity, his/her moral development, ability to change, and so on, pushed concepts of subjectivity further and further as the recesses of consciousness were extended and explored. This was reinforced by the growth of the science of psychology in the late nineteenth and early twentieth centuries which became a very powerful discourse; for Freud and his followers reality was all the more firmly located in the individual, if in regions buried in the psyche which were difficult to uncover. From an Althusserian point of view though, such approaches further reinforce the ideology of the subject in heightening the illusion of individualism. This perhaps explains why Freud's theories enjoyed much more popularity in the early twentieth century and were much more rapidly institutionalized than those of Marx, which could not so easily be shaped to or be assimilated by the dominant ideology and its myths.

Psychoanalytic approaches

The influence of Freudian and associated psychoanalytical theory has been very widespread culturally, not only in a formal sense but in that the discourse of psychoanalysis has permeated most forms of western knowledge and ways of thinking in the twentieth century to some extent: it has been normalized as a way of understanding the mind. In literary theory, which has arisen in a post-Freudian age, it would be impossible not to take account of such ideas even if only to reject them. Freud himself, as with Marx, used literature to develop and illustrate some of his theories; the 'Oedipus complex' is one of the best known examples which has become ingrained in popular consciousness. Freud's model of the individual psyche, with *conscious, subconscious* or *preconscious*, and *unconscious* levels of activity has proved very influential. This is particularly because it lays claim to discovering an area of activity which is hidden from us in our everyday lives but which contains a kind of determining reality, the *unconscious*: a region in which we hide or repress our deepest desires and fears that can only manifest itself through symbolic ways in dreaming, parapraxes or Freudian slips, or the lengthy process of psychoanalysis itself. In suggesting that life at a conscious level is a kind of disguise or surface form of existence which is controlled by the immanent forces contained in the concept of the unconscious, Freudianism perhaps ironically has much in common with Marxism's concept of ideology; as theories or philosophies they are usually seen as antithetical in most respects although some recent literary theory has synthesized aspects from both, for example Fredric Jameson sees ideology in literary texts as a form of 'political unconscious'. Freud's later model of personality (1923) as consisting of the *superego*, the *ego* and the *id* has also had a powerful effect on conceptions of character for both writers and critics, together with the identification of the *pleasure principle* or the sexual drive of *eros* as a fundamental force which determines many human actions including those of writing and reading. We should note though that Freud's ideas did change considerably, and writers and critics have often used his work selectively; there are several 'Freuds', and as with Marxism, Freudian theory is still a developing body of knowledge.

Freud's theories have been especially influential in literary criticism and instrumental in the development in some areas of literary theory for a number of reasons. First because Freudian theory attempts to provide universal models and explanations for the drives which underpin the way people behave: the concepts of *desire* and *pleasure* have been theorized in terms of writing and reading extensively in recent years. This is closely linked to Freud's theory of the development of the individual and the various phases of arousal and awareness which he/she passes through. Secondly, Freud offers ways of interpreting the manner in which desire and pleasure, and other aspects of the psyche, manifest themselves. In particular, the ways in which Freud interpreted dreams in stressing *symbolism*, and the related phenomena of *displacement* and *condensation*. These had a particular effect on Modernist writing in the early twentieth century and later encouraged ways of reading which looked for meanings beyond the apparent or the literal. In a sense Freud allowed the critic more freedom and creativity than hitherto, permitting and validating interpretations which had previously been unavailable. To take an example already used, episodes in *Mansfield Park* take on new meanings in the light of Freudian theory so that the episode where Fanny resists going through the iron gates into the wilderness can acquire a more specifically sexual significance (namely repression) than had been possible before. William Empson's analysis of episodes in *Alice's Adventures in Wonderland* (1865) in *Some Versions of Pastoral* (1935) is a good example of Freudian criticism in full flow:

> To make the dream-story from which *Wonderland* was elaborated seem Freudian one only has to tell it. A fall through a deep hole into the secrets of Mother Earth produces a new enclosed soul wondering who it is, what will be its position in the world, and how it will get out . . . . The nightmare

theme of the birth-trauma, that she grows too big for the room and is almost crushed by it .... Alice peering through the hole into the garden may be wanting a return to the womb as well as an escape from it[24]

The publication of Joseph Conrad's *Heart of Darkness* (1899) coincides with the circulation of Freud's theories on dreams, which were to be published as *The Interpretation of Dreams* (1900). The complex symbolism, ambiguity and dislocated patterning of *Heart of Darkness* bear a close resemblance to dreams, the nature and functioning of which are discussed by Freud, and the text readily lends itself to psychoanalytic interpretation. By *condensation* in dreams Freud meant the ways in which an image or word can acquire a number of meanings, so that we compress several concepts through association into one figure or image which it may be hard to decipher. An example of this in a literary text is the moment early in *Heart of Darkness* where the anonymous narrator talks of the group of people sitting on the deck of the boat playing dominoes as 'toying architecturally with the bones'. The word 'bones' seems rather odd at this stage of the text, but we come to realize that it carries a number of associations which converge symbolically in the course of the narrative. Dominoes were made from ivory, which becomes a symbol for the source of the wealth which supports the characters of the lawyer and the accountant, here innocently playing with the carved pieces. But it also merges with images later in the text of skeletons with grass sprouting between the bones, which in turn merges with images of a capital city with grass growing up between the paving stones, combining to form a complex set of ideas which is hard to unravel and explain rationally or consciously. Certainly it combines the ideas to suggest the corpse of capitalism, but in ways which the characters are unaware of and which the reader has to discover through hidden associations. The effect is produced by the powerful compression or condensation of images as in a dream; indeed Marlow as narrator of his own tale breaks off to reflect on it saying:

> It seems to me I am trying to tell you a dream - making a vain attempts, because no relation of a dream can convey the dream–sensation, that commingling of absurdity, surprise, and bewilderment in tremor of struggling revolt, that notion of being captured by the incredible which is of the very essence of dreams.[25]

Displacement can often work with *condensation*, according to Freud's explanations of dreams; again it works to reveal the hidden or latent meaning below the surface or manifest level of dream narratives. Through *displacement*, a figure or concept is transformed into an apparently unrelated image which allows the otherwise inexpressible or repressed element to be represented in disguised form. The dream, in other words, can be interpreted as showing the dreamer aspects of his or her unconscious mind, though in a way which is indirect and manageable. Literary texts can be read along similar lines; the transformation of Gregor Samsa into an insect in Kafka's *Metamorphosis* allows a number of readings which are expressed through this extended central metaphor. *Condensation* and *displacement* have been linked to Jakobson's language poles of *metaphor* and *metonymy* respectively, the former working through similarity shifts and the latter through contiguity shifts. This view of literary texts as a kind of code, and as ways of saying what other discourses cannot say or will not allow to be said, has been very influential in literary theory and criticism. It also reinforces by another route the privileged position which literature occupies or lays claim to. Psychoanalysis is a powerful form of knowledge which can be used to 'explain' literary texts, in effect allowing the reader to become the analyst and the text the object of analysis or analysand, thus privileging psychoanalysis as a discourse above that of the literary text and conferring on the reader a superior position. However, this relationship is questionable and can be modified, and this takes us back to the role of the reader.

As we have seen, the act of reading has acquired a much more important position through literary theory, and if we parallel the reader's position with that of psychoanalyst, then one of the dangers we need to recognize is in what Freud called *transference* and *countertransference*. By the term *transference*, Freud indicated how we invest people with various qualities, both good and bad, at an unconscious level, and how in turn an awareness of this in the person in question can lead to a response or countertransference, and so on. The relationship between patient and psychoanalyst is subject to the same processes, and consequently psychoanalysis is usually seen as a two-way or dialectical process in which not only is the patient being analysed but also by implication the analyst through the very dependent relationship they build: it has been demonstrated that the analysand may produce dreams especially for the analyst which will inevitably bring about a projection of the analyst's own desires or fears onto the patient. In the same way, the reading act should be seen as a two-way or *dialogic* process whereby not only the text is read but the reader also. Meanings thus do not arise only from the text or only from the reader but through interaction and collaboration of both: it is a totally interdependent relationship. We need to take into account the manipulations of and struggles for desire and power which arise both in literary texts and the reading of them. In other words, in Freudian terms reading can be seen as an unfolding of our own consciousness and unconsciousness as well as that of the text: recognizing the forms of resistance and finding the points at which they can be unlocked leads to a deeper understanding of text and reader. A further dimension of this interplay between psychoanalysis and literature is to grant literature its right to interpret psychoanalysis: as with all forms of knowledge they are also systems of language or discourses with their own narrative and rhetorical structures. These do differ significantly and as a consequence so do the relations between them and the kinds of power they exert, and our position as reader, or as an individual subject, is composed of a combination of these in various relations which are or should be open to change and redefinition. Reading is a major form of self-redefinition and the interaction of literary and psychoanalytic discourses can help us to understand this process.

Freud's identification of *pleasure* as a central motivation in human behaviour has been developed in psychoanalytical and linguistic literary theory together with the concept of *desire*. The theories are too complex to write on in any detail here, although some mention of their significance and application is helpful by way of introduction. Freud saw pleasure or the *pleasure principle* as central to human development: the desire for physical or sexual gratification and then the control or repression of these desires in the child's recognition of the *reality principle* are fundamental to the formation of the human psyche in terms of the *id/ego/superego* model whereby instinctual drives are controlled largely through a process of socialization. Allied to this is the recognition of gender whereby the male child becomes aware of his penis and the female of its absence. Freud's theories on gender have arguably reinforced male and female stereotyping, and been criticized in particular by some feminist theorists, although feminist theory has also developed Freudian ideas, as we shall see shortly. Freud sees the Oedipus complex as the key to the male child's entry into the adult world of reality where the sexual desire for his mother is repressed through the fear of castration by the father. At this stage the male child becomes aware of gender, and is initiated into the masculine roles which reinforce what we can call the patriarchal order. The female child on the other hand has to come to terms with her lack of maleness and to repress in turn her desire to seduce her father; identification with her mother and the substitution of baby for penis are, according to Freud, the female equivalent to the male's experience of the Oedipus complex. Now at one level the 'truth' of Freud's theories does perhaps seem questionable: how can these hypotheses be tested? Where is the evidence for the unconscious? But in another way they have as language and narratives which circulate in society, *ipso facto* become 'true'. They are ingrained in various spheres of public consciousness and inescapable in the effects they have. Whether Freud discovered or created the unconscious is in fact a redundant question: Freudian theory as a discourse inscribes it in our culture indelibly and ineluctably.

The power of Freudian language as discourse is an appropriate point at which to introduce one of the main developments of Freud's theories. The French theorist Jacques Lacan views language as the major force in shaping human identity: through language the individual gains his or her subject positions. Language allows a range of relational positions into which the human subject or individual is drawn. Submission to language is also submission to patriarchal authority, and with this comes awareness of self as opposed to the undifferentiated, pre-linguistic and unconscious state of being which the child experiences. This is a refinement of Freud's concept of the shift from the pleasure principle to the reality principle. Lacan links Freud's theory to Saussure's linguistic theory; his own theories of the unconscious and language are complex and can only be described here in brief outline. He sees the unconscious as structured by language, but consisting of language only at the level of the *signifier*, not the *signified*. In this respect, the unconscious allows for the free play of language as sign before it is trained into specific, fixed meanings or signifieds through conscious processes. Related to this is Lacan's model of the construction of the individual subject in childhood which passes through two crucial stages. The first of these is the 'mirror' stage which occurs at about 6 months when the child becomes aware of his or her image in a mirror. This, argues Lacan, is peculiar to humans who become fascinated with their reflection and see it as an object which they aspire to as an image of a unified self which is seen from outside and which offers a sense of identity and difference from the world which surrounds it. The second stage occurs about a year later and marks the point of entry into society and, conversely, the entry of society's language into the child: what Lacan calls the 'symbolic order'. This reinforces the two-way state of the mirror stage in that the child has to adopt a language outside itself, an image of itself is conferred by borrowing a language which exists outside of itself. In using terms such as 'I' and 'me' or 'myself', society's language is used to give a sense of individual identity. The point here is that language functions as a control system which in normal social practice it is hard to resist. Most institutionalized discourses reinforce the ways in which any free play or slippage of meaning or identity are prevented or resisted. I deliberately referred to the child as 'it' suggesting an ungendered being, but as we have already seen, language is not neutral with respect to gender and normally privileges the male position. For Lacan, as with Freud, patriarchal order is represented by the phallus and language is *phallocentric* or structured around the controlling centre of the symbolic phallus. Lacan sees the child acquiring an identity within the symbolic order which is either male or female. Male identity is constructed in positive terms as the norm, female identity in negative ways as the 'other', as lacking a phallus and thus negatively differentiated.

The implications of this for literature and literary theory are that the psyche and human identity are seen in terms of their linguistic construction, in effect in *textual* terms. Although arising from a different body of theoretical knowledge, there are certainly elements of similarity between the kind of view of the individual subject in Althusser's work as positioned and determined by illusory ideological processes and that of Lacan stemming from Freud, whereby the individual is taken over, so to speak, in the process of his or her integration into society. Literary texts can be seen as contributing to or reflecting these processes: the function of character, certainly in many nineteenth-century novels, is to bestow an acceptable identity on human subjects. Again *Great Expectations* provides a good example in the way that Pip acquires a moral language which can cope with the economic forces operating in society. The individual subject is thus a product of discourse: discursively constructed and held in place. There are though texts which question or fracture such constructions of individual identity: Sylvia Plath's *The Bell Jar* (1963) is a good example of the ways in which a female subject, Esther, is constantly subjected to pressures which are largely exerted through language to behave in certain ways and assume a particular identity based on her gender and class positions:

> I also remembered Buddy Willard saying in a sinister, knowing way that after I had had children I would feel differently, I wouldn't want to write poems any more. So I began to think maybe it was true that when you were married and had children it was like being brainwashed, and afterwards you went about numb as a slave in some private, totalitarian state.[26]

Her resistance to this is diagnosed as mental illness: her inability to conform to what appear as social norms is read by those in positions of power as abnormal, deviant behaviour.

Psychoanalytic theory can extend beyond the study of character though; it can offer broader ways of reading texts as a whole, and of understanding their formal construction. A literary text can be viewed as a kind of model of the psyche in that certain control systems together with different levels of consciousness or meaning can be discovered. We might perhaps see literature as a kind of *superego* or alternatively as an expression of repressed desires and fears in the unconscious; certain kinds of texts, especially those we might consider as modernist, can be read more multivalently and do not have to be placed in a fixed system of meaning. The signifiers of the text, especially if it is a text without a central controlling narrative discourse, can produce a free play of meaning as in dreams. Kafka's *Metamorphosis* resists fixed or normative interpretation; indeed meaning seems to be relentlessly postponed or deferred: there is no complete or satisfactory explanation for Gregor Samsa's transformation into an insect and the ensuing action. It is in fact a text which can be interpreted as an expression of the death wish emanating from the unconscious; Freud modified his view that the main human drive is sexual in *Beyond the Pleasure Principle* (1920) in which he identified *thanatos* or a wish for death as the ultimate desire because all the tensions in the human psyche disappeared in this final state of non-being. Gregor's happiness seems to increase as he gets closer to death and in his absence there is a sense of well-being at the end of the text, whereby a postponement of any final meaning or closure is achieved.

Certainly literary texts can be seen as what we could call control systems, in terms of narrative method, character construction and positioning, and the arrangement of the various discourses usually present. The marginalizing or silencing of particular voices, for example the first 'mad' Mrs Rochester in *Jane Eyre* (1847), or the representation of militant and Trade Union politics in Dickens's *Hard Times* in the grotesque figure of Slackbridge, reveal much about how literary texts are formed and how they organize or negotiate the surrounding historical discourses which they draw on.

Notes

1 See Raymond Williams, *Keywords* (London, Fontana, 1976), pp. 60–9.
2 Karl Marx, Preface to *A Contribution to the Critique of Political Economy*, in *Marx and Engels: Selected Works Vol. I* (London, Lawrence & Wishart, 1968), p. 181. First published in 1859.

3 The emergence of Cultural Studies as an academic field began in the 1960s, and it soon established itself as a separate field of interdisciplinary studies; the two most influential figures in forming this area in Britain were Raymond Williams and Richard Hoggart, the latter setting up the Centre for Contemporary Cultural Studies at Birmingham University in 1964 as an extension of the English Department. Although drawing on a wide range of theoretical positions, in particular Marxist thought and especially Gramsci's theory of hegemony, and applying these to a diverse range of textual and social phenomena, Cultural Studies has retained a close relationship to the discipline of English and arguably done much to reinvigorate it both theoretically and in its objects of study, bringing popular and working-class literature into the curriculum. In some institutions now, the boundary between Cultural Studies and English is virtually indiscernible. (See Antony Easthope, *Literary into Cultural Studies* (London, Routledge, 1991) for a discussion of the relationship between English and Cultural Studies.)

4 Raymond Williams, *Marxism and Literature* (Oxford, Oxford University Press, 1977), p. 110.

5 Robert Tressell, *The Ragged Trousered Philanthropists* (London, Granada, 1965), pp. 352–3. First published in abridged form in 1914, and in complete form in 1955.

6 Michel Foucault, interview in *The History of Sexuality* (London, Allen Lane, 1978).

7 Ralph Fox, *The Novel and the People* (London, Lawrence & Wishart, 1979), p. 104. First published in 1937.

8 Lucien Goldmann, *The Hidden God* (London, Routledge, 1964), p.17. First published in France in 1959.

9 Terry Eagleton, 'Form, Ideology and *The Secret Agent*', in *Against the Grain: Selected Essays 1975–1985* (London, Verso, 1986). First published in 1978.

10 Simone de Beauvoir, *The Second Sex* (Harmondsworth, Penguin, 1987), p. 16. First published in France in 1949.

11 Annette Kolodny, 'Dancing Through the Minefield: Some Observations on the Theory, Practice, and Politics of a Feminist Literary Criticism', in Elaine Showalter, ed., *The New Feminist Criticism: Essays on Women, Literature and Theory* (London, Virago, 1986), p. 153. First published in America in 1985.

12 Dale Spender, *Man Made Language* (London, Routledge, 1980), p.23.

13 Dale Spender, *Invisible Women: the Schooling Scandal* (London, Writers and Readers, 1982), p.2.

14 Cora Kaplan, *Sea Changes: Culture and Feminism* (London, Verso, 1986), p.162.

15 Toril Moi, *Sexual/Textual Politics: Feminist Literary Theory* (London, Methuen, 1985), p. 78.

16 Virginia Woolf, *Orlando* (Harmondsworth, Penguin, 1942), pp. 97–8. First published in 1928.

17 Judith Butler, *Gender Trouble: Feminism and the Subversion of Identity* (London, Routledge, 1990), Preface / ix.

18 Marjorie Garber, *Vested Interests: Cross-Dressing and Cultural Anxiety* (London, Routledge, 1992), p. 17.

19 Marjorie Garber, *op. cit.*, p. 10.

20 Diana Fuss, ed., *Introduction to Inside/Out: Lesbian Theories, Gay Theories* (London, Routledge, 1991), p. 3.

21 Jonathan Dollimore, *Sexual Disidence: Augustine to Wilde, Freud to Foucault* (Oxford, Oxford University Press,1991), p. 21.

22 Louis Althusser, 'Ideology and Ideological State Apparatuses', in *Lenin and Philosophy and Other Essays* (New York/London, Monthly Review Press, 1971), pp. 171–2. First published in France in 1970.

23 Robin Wood, 'Levin and the Jam', in *Personal Views: Explorations in Film* (London, Gordon Fraser, 1979).

24 William Empson, *Some Versions of Pastoral* (London, Chatto and Windus, 1986), p.271. First published in 1935.

25 Joseph Conrad, *Heart of Darkness* (Harmondsworth, Penguin, 1983), p.57. First published in 1899.

26 Sylvia Plath, *The Bell Jar* (London, Faber & Faber, 1966), p. 89. First published in 1963.

5 Textual relations

So far we have looked at a range of theoretical approaches to literary texts and critical practice. Some of these offer very different ways of reading and thinking about literature, different that is from traditional approaches which are largely untheorized. We should not envisage the area of literary theory as forming a unified body of knowledge; to do this would be to attempt to organicize and harmonize the very forms of complexity, contradiction and difference which theoretical approaches reveal as underlying the whole institution of literature and literary studies. However, theory should not be seen as a series of discrete or mutually exclusive positions either. As we have seen, various approaches share their origins in linguistic theory, especially Saussure's theory of the sign, and apparently diverse conceptions of the individual and society arising from Freudian and Marxist theories share some elements. What these approaches also have in common is that they reveal that a text has no one meaning or that there needs to be an accepted, normative way of reading. Texts will produce different meanings according to the conditions or contexts in which they are read or consumed.

Hamlet is a text which is constantly being reinterpreted: the limits of its meaning cannot be determined because the contexts in which it is read, performed or written about are always subject to change. In this sense, the proliferation of meanings and the range of interpretations available should ensure that literary studies and criticism are enduring activities, not because they contain timeless and universal truths but because they point to the changing nature of meaning and the conditions which give rise to these meanings. As long as we conceive of history and social processes as involving change and forms of difference, then literary interpretation will be involved in these processes and subject to debate and alteration. We have already considered the importance of the literary work as *text*, drawing attention to language and structure together with the reader's role as a more active agent in the reading process than some traditional kinds of literary criticism had allowed for. In this final chapter I want to look at some theories of *textuality*, and then to consider some of the ways in which texts are located in larger networks of interpretation.

Theories of textuality

Roland Barthes' concept of the literary text in his essays 'The Death of the Author' and 'From Work to Text' has already been introduced. Barthes' ideas though are part of a larger redefinition of the idea of a literary work, or for that matter of any kind of document, although these kinds of approach are more usually associated with what we think of as 'literary' writing. In semiotics, that is the study of signs and the production of meaning from them, òr in linguistics, a *text* is defined as a body of signs constituting a message which has an existence independent from its author or sender and its reader or receiver. By 'existence' the physical aspect of the text is indicated; there is no sense in which a text gives rise to meaning separate from its reading or reception, as we have already seen when considering the limitations of formalist approaches. Barthes' view of the literary text as composed of 'multiple writings' which come from a wide range of sources and exist in relations of 'contestation' rather than coalescing into a smooth and integrated whole is a crucial departure from the organiscist conception of literary works. It suggests that a text consists of an uneasy assemblage of various strands which interact in different and perhaps unpredictable ways.

In his book *S/Z* (1970), Barthes classifies literary texts into two categories, what he calls *readerly* and *writerly* texts. The former is the kind of text which leaves the reader as a passive consumer, which has what Barthes calls a 'negative, reactive value: what can be read but not written'; such a text, a 'classic text' he states, plunges the reader into a state of idleness. The *writerly* text though makes the reader 'no longer a consumer, but the producer of the text'; in other words the reader is activated and in effect becomes the writer of the text. The Italian theorist Umberto Eco has a similar set of categories in what he terms *closed* and *open* texts, the former being as the term suggests a text in which the reading experience is restrictive whereas the latter offers a range of possibilities of interpretation. Barthes also asserts though that the text is *plural*: it cannot be reduced to a single meaning – it is irreducible, and here he makes no distinction between 'writerly' and 'readerly' texts. Barthes in fact exemplifies this in his own writing; in

S/Z he discusses Balzac's short story *Sarrasine* (1830) which represents a readerly or classic text, but his reading of the story is so rich and productive that even a text which might appear resistant to a plural or open reading does, given the reader, offer complex and multiple meanings. Barthes sees the text as a *network* both in terms of its internal structures of meaning and also in the ways in which it combines with the external frameworks in which it is situated. He proposes a model of interpretation along the lines of Einsteinian relativity, so that 'the relativity of the frames of reference be included in the object studied': there is now a recognition that the positions from which a text is read will determine its meanings. Barthes frequently uses metaphors of 'weaving', 'tissue', 'texture', 'strands' and 'filiation' when talking about the structure of texts. He dismisses the traditional idea of the text as a 'veil' behind which is concealed a definitive meaning waiting to be revealed. Instead the text is a surface over which the reader can range in any number of ways that the text permits. In this Barthes abandons the idea of the text possessing a final 'secret, an ultimate meaning'; the traditional 'depth' model as we might call it where such a meaning is to be discovered is replaced by what we could call the 'surface' model : 'the space of writing is to be ranged over, not pierced'. He sees this as revolutionary because it is an 'anti-theological activity': in other words such interpretive strategies refuse to acknowledge a fixed meaning and thus liberate the text. Such readings however are, as Barthes recognizes, dependent on the reader and the context or framework in which the text is read. This process has been theorized by Barthes and others and the term frequently applied to it is *intertextuality*.

Intertextuality

The concept of the *intertext* arises in France in the late 1960s, and has become increasingly significant as a way of thinking about how a literary text is produced and comes to acquire meanings. Barthes' view of the text as a *network* helps partly to explain what is meant by the term. We have already seen how the figure of the author is no longer considered as central to a text's production or meaning: the author has been decentred in the interpretive process. Instead, a text consists of multiple writings, and writings which are drawn from a range of discourses, already in circulation in some form or other. If anything, the writer is not thought of as the great originator, the creative genius, but rather a synthesizer: someone who draws together and orchestrates linguistic raw materials. In this sense, literature becomes a form of repetition to an extent. An example would be the ways in which certain narratives, those which we call myths especially, keep recurring in modified forms: the Oedipus story would be indicative of this as variants of it keep appearing across literary history. The repeated use of the 'Grail' or quest motif in chivalric and Arthurian legends from Malory to T.H. White, and variations on this in other narratives such as Rider Haggard's *King Solomon's Mines* (1886), Joseph Conrad's *Heart of Darkness* and Francis Ford Coppola's film *Apocalypse Now* (1979), or T.S. Eliot's *The Waste Land*, indicate the ways in which a particular story or myth can be repeated in different ways. More specific instances would be the way in which *Jane Eyre* is clearly reworked in Daphne DuMaurier's Rebecca (1936) and very self-consciously rewritten from the point of view of the first Mrs Rochester in Jean Rhys's *Wide Sargasso Sea* (1966); in the latter instance it is as if the text makes explicit the process of repetition which occurs more implicitly in all forms of literary production, as does Tom Stoppard's *Rosencrantz and Guildenstern are Dead* (1967) in relation to *Hamlet*, albeit very significantly modified. John Fowles' *The French Lieutenant's Woman* (1969) contains many quotations from historical, sociological, biological, geographical and literary texts which are self-consciously woven into the narrative as well as more indirect allusions to nineteenth- and twentieth-century fictional conventions.

Thomas Hardy, not usually thought of as an experimental novelist, recognized this kind of process:

> What has been written cannot be blotted. Each new style of novel must be the old with added ideas, not an ignoring and avoidance of the old. And so of religion, and a good many other things![1]

Hardy's fiction is of course very repetitive in several respects, and his final novel *The Well-Beloved* (1897) can be read as a self-conscious recognition both of Hardy's reworking of the same narratives and a more general pattern of repetition in art across history. A helpful metaphor which Hardy uses in various contexts is of a *palimpsest,* that is a writing surface such as a wax tablet on which the original has been partially or wholly reworked, written over successively. Barthes makes this point in his essay 'Theory of the Text':

> Any text is a new tissue of past citations. Bits of codes, formulae, rhythmic models, fragments of social languages, etc. pass into the text and are redistributed within it, for there is always language before and around the text.[2]

Literary textuality then can be seen as a kind of discursive recycling, although the new relations which come to exist between the discourses appropriated and incorporated into a text ensure that literary writing is never the same, never completely repeated. T.S. Eliot's poem *The Waste Land* or James Joyce's novel *Ulysses* are good illustrations of texts which self-consciously rework eclectic ranges of literary and other discourses already in circulation which are to a greater or lesser extent recognizable, but which come to assume a quite different status as they are incorporated into new combinations and juxtapositions. It is significant that Eliot published a set of explanatory notes with *The Waste Land* which locate it in frames of reference external to the text of the poem, and much of the critical scholarship on *Ulysses* has been concerned with locating the novel in the wider narratives and structures of knowledge which are woven into the text. The American critic Harold Bloom in *The Anxiety of Influence: A Theory of Poetry* (1973) sees the desire to evade earlier writing as a central motivation in literary production. In the cases of Eliot and Joyce, it is as if they recognized this process of literature being a reflection of itself to an extent. In reading *Ulysses,* an increased significance is gained if Joyce's earlier, and indeed later fiction has also been read: there are sets of cross references and allusions which, to use a traditional term, provide a 'richer' reading experience or – to employ theoretical terms – the signifiers in the text evoke more complex signifieds. A knowledge of the character of Stephen Dedalus gained from *A Portrait of the Artist as a Young Man*, and also from an earlier version of this, *Stephen Hero* (1944), which was only published after Joyce's death (which also raises interesting questions about chronology and intentionality), provides one frame of reference from which to approach *Ulysses*; it is of course one of the more conventional and institutionalized ways of studying literature through a detailed knowledge of one author's works.

When we read a text though, consciously or unconsciously we place it in wider frames of reference of language and knowledge than those to do with a particular author, period or set of literary criteria. In a sense, we 'cover' the text with a multiplicity of discourses drawn from our own culture and experience which will vary according to time, place and the individual reader. Barthes in an essay called 'Criticism as Language' (1963) examines the nature of criticism and sees its function not as a way of discovering 'truths', that is for Philosophy to determine, but to find forms of 'validity':

> We might say that the task of criticism ... is purely formal: it does not consist in 'discovering' in the work or the author under consideration

something 'hidden' or 'profound' or 'secret' which has so far escaped notice (through what miracle? Are we more perceptive than our predecessors?) but only in *fitting together* – as a skilled cabinet maker, by a process of intelligent fumbling, interlocks two parts of a complicated piece of furniture – the language of the day (Existentialism, Marxism or psychoanalysis) and the language of the author, that is, the formal system of logical rules that he evolved in the conditions of his time ... . If there is such a thing as critical proof, it lies not in the ability to *discover* the work under consideration but, on the contrary, to cover it as completely as possible with one's own language.[3]

Barthes sees criticism here then as a kind of alignment between the language of the text and the language used to read and interpret it. Such alignments will change for a range of reasons. As Antony Easthope puts it, 'the text has an identity, but that identity is always relational';[4] he illustrates this by suggesting that a text which may have defamiliarized its readers in 1912 may not do so, or at least not in the same way, in 1922. Reading conditions change as literary forms change, and *vice versa*. Tony Bennett takes up a similar position in his concept of 'reading formations': 'a set of intersecting discourses which productively activate a given body of texts and the relations between them in a specific way'.[5] Bennett develops this interpretive model from Michel Foucault's description of a book or text in his highly influential work *The Archaeology of Knowledge* (1969):

The frontiers of a book are never clear-cut: beyond the title, the first line and the last full-stop, beyond its internal configuration, its autonomous form, it is caught up in a system of references to other books, other texts, other sentences ... The book is simply not the object that one holds in one's hands ... its unity is variable and relative.[6]

For Bennett, a text is 'constantly *rewritten* into a variety of different material, social, institutional and ideological contexts'.

The idea of texts being *rewritten* through the reading and interpretive processes, which has already been raised by other theorists, is a helpful way of thinking about intertextuality. There is a very good illustration of this in a short story by Jorge Luis Borges called 'Pierre Menard, Author of the *Quixote*' (1964). In this narrative, it transpires that a twentieth-century novelist, Pierre Menard, had set himself the task of rewriting Cervantes' *Don Quixote* (1605–15) word for word. This is undertaken not by reconstructing the conditions under which Cervantes wrote in the early seventeenth century and writing as if he were Cervantes, which Menard rejects as too easy, but by remaining a twentieth-century novelist and writing the *Quixote* through these contemporary experiences. Menard succeeds in his project to the extent of (re)writing two and a bit chapters word for word before he dies, and the narrator quotes from this 'new' text and the original *Quixote* by Cervantes. The quotations are of course identical, but the narrator makes the point that they are entirely different in their meanings. The phrase '... truth, whose mother is history,' can be read in entirely different ways depending on its historical context. In the seventeenth century it is 'mere rhetorical praise of history'. In the twentieth century it can be read that history 'is not an enquiry into reality but its origin': historical truth 'is not what has happened; it is what we judge to have happened'. The story serves as a kind of allegory for literary production and consumption, and illustrates the concept of intertextuality through fictional discourse. In a sense, all texts undergo a process of *rewriting* as they are reread, reproduced; reading and interpretation could, following the palimpsest metaphor, be thought of as reinscription. Tony Bennett prefers the phrase 'productive activation' to 'interpretation' in that reading in its fullest historical sense involves a series of meanings consciously activated between text and reader.

A further complexity that we need to remind ourselves of however is that any act of reconstruction we perform in which we try to imagine the conditions of production – the context in which a text was written, or later contexts or moments of interpretation, are themselves forms of projection from the reading context necessarily involving specula-tion. If we try to read *Hamlet* from an imagined early seventeenth-century point of view when it was first produced, or again in a 1930s context, the knowledge with which we surround *Hamlet* in each case could be a variety of sources from historical accounts of the periods, biographical material, accounts by members of the audience, photographs or sketches, and so on, and these too are texts which we arrange around the text which is the object of study and the meanings which we produce from these in order to interpret *Hamlet* in a particular way are themselves subject to and determined by the conditions in which they are read. This turns reading into potentially endlessly regressive planes of relativity, and there are strong theoret-ical and critical debates and divisions over the extent to which such a relativised approach can become ultimately pointless and meaning-less. This leads into the area known as *deconstruction* which has figured prominently in much recent theoretical writing, and has been especially influential in some American academic institutions.

Deconstructing the text

The French theorist Jacques Derrida, who is usually thought of as the main founder of the movement known as *deconstruction*, argued in 'Structure, Sign and Play in the Discourses of the Human Sciences' (1966) that in western science and philosophy forms of knowledge are structured around a *centre*, and that this structuring process does not normally draw attention to itself: it has become naturalized. Discourse or knowledge usually refers to a centre, to 'a point of presence, a fixed origin'.[7] The function of this centre is, according to Derrida, twofold. It provides a focus, and allows knowledge to be organized around a certain truth or revelation which presents itself as absolute: a pattern which traditional critical approaches to literary texts often reinforce in offering what claim to be definitive interpretations, as do other forms of discourse such as legal judgements or medical diagnoses. It also crucially functions to limit, or delimit the meanings available; to circumscribe or contain the ways in which a text or field of knowledge can be understood, so that any proliferation or free play of meaning is prevented. Meaning is contained within the system of knowledge so that a discourse makes or validates its own truth and does not draw attention to the ways in which this is achieved. The growth of what have become known as academic 'disciplines' is an important feature of the historical process by which a series of discursive fields became relatively autonomous and self-contained, so that literary 'truths' were assessed solely in terms of literary-critical criteria which could identify and assess such forms of 'truthfulness'; historical 'truth' in similar fashion is constructed through criteria determined by philosophers of history, and so on. Knowledge becomes in this way self-validating. Indeed one feature of the language of knowledge is its tautological nature, saying the same thing if by somewhat different means. This is not to suggest that these discursive fields function totally independently from each other, that they are mutually exclusive. Aspects of history are often used to reinforce literary study for example, and disciplines share, according to Derrida's model, similar overall forms of structuration so that the forms of knowledge are shared, if not the contents. There is, in other words, a kind of self-sufficiency about knowledge as it is organized into its particular categories.

For Derrida, the key element of this process is what he terms *logocentrism*, that is the metaphysics of presence or the essential meanings that supposedly exist prior to language and therefore beyond a text as being central or fundamental to meaning and knowledge in western culture. Deconstruction involves the dismantling of such an authoritative position; Derrida's statement that 'there is nothing outside of the text' is an attempt to overthrow this belief, indicating that it is only the text itself which speaks, not some prior and external origin or presence. *Centres* of meaning can be identified from the 'I' of our own sense of individual identity, to more collective centres of nationhood; for example, English literature has been instrumental in constructing the myth of 'Englishness' so fundamental to the country's cultural identity. Western religion is centred on the idea of God with a series of orbiting subcentres which function to hold the ultimate centre of being or *presence* in place. When a centre is questioned or modified, as with Freud's redefinition of the psyche so that the traditional model of the mind and consciousness is displaced by the concept of the unconscious, a new centre is in turn constructed. It seems impossible to think, speak or write without involving some sort of underlying *centrism* in our discourse. Language has been historically invested with powers of *presence*: Derrida argues that Plato's privileging of the spoken over the written word was one way of investing language with authenticity, fixing it with a specific origin and thus anchoring it to a particular moment with a certain meaning.[8] The same has happened with much written language in explaining texts largely in terms of their authors' intentions, and locating writing in institutional networks or frames of reference which seek to hold their meanings in place. Derrida suggests that meaning is never in fact single or fixed, but constantly proliferating and shifting or slipping, whether it be in spoken or written language. He terms this scattering and flickering of meanings which potentially arise from any kind of text *dissemination.*

Derrida's term for conceptualizing how meaning works and which underpins the project of deconstruction is *différance*; he uses this in the French sense of the word which itself helps to indicate its meaning. '*Différance*' translates first of all as 'difference' in a sense derived from Saussure's view of language as a system of differences, that is we are able to distinguish between words and their associated meanings through a system of sound differences and by understanding that one thing is not another thing. So that 'dog' is not 'bog' or 'hog', or even 'umbrella' or 'parasol'. For Saussure the relationship between *signifier* and *signified* was a stable one, the system of phonetic and semantic differences worked in a regulated and unproblematic way. But for Derrida it becomes highly problematic: meaning is always in a state of contention and flux. When we think of 'dog' we are also thinking about what it is not: not a cat, hog or whatever. In other words when we try to fix a meaning, to represent something as singular, positive, authoritative, we achieve this by silencing or negating those different or opposite figures or meanings which it is situated against. We cannot have the idea of 'good' without its opposite 'evil', we cannot have the idea of 'man' and 'maleness' without 'woman' and 'womanliness'. The more strongly a particular meaning or value is articulated, the more significant are the areas of difference which surround it. In this sense, Derrida argues that texts are really about what they appear *not* to be about, and he searches for weak points, or fractures where the *otherness* that texts conceal become apparent. We might take *Mansfield Park* again as an example and note that sexual desire is never explicitly mentioned although it is arguably a constant threat to the kind of social order and marital relations which are constructed as normal and moral. But the scene where Fanny is left sitting outside the gates to the wilderness into which other characters trespass seems to set in motion the possibility of sexual desire; sexual affairs are a taboo, unspoken subject in the text, at most alluded to, but they are essential to hold in place the surface moral order. In a sense, the subject of *Mansfield Park* is just as much immorality as it is morality, but the immoral remains unmentionable and silent, and by doing so determines the language and behaviour of morality. This kind of fracture which reveals the *otherness* of meaning Derrida terms *aporia*: in Greek 'doubt' or 'perplexity'. Some texts, he argues, reveal their 'otherness' and the ways in which meaning is constructed and 'centred' self-consciously whereby the inherent contradictions on which they are based become apparent. This is especially the case with certain literary texts which may, unlike other forms of discourse, foreground not only meaning but the ways in which meaning is produced. Clearly this has quite a lot in common with other theoretical approaches to literary texts which we have already encountered through Bakhtin and Barthes.

Derrida's other sense of *différance* is 'deferment', which arises from the French 'différer' meaning 'to defer' as well as 'to differ'. The idea that meaning is never complete, never fully realized but always just beyond us, postponed or deferred, is indicated here. Words are defined by other words, which are in turn defined by other words, so that we can never come to a point of fully realized, non-regressive meaning. It is rather like Lewis Carroll's playing with the meaning of meaning in *Alice's Adventures in Wonderland* (1865): when Alice is told by the March Hare 'Then you should say what you mean' and she replies 'I mean what I say – that's the same thing, you know', to which the Hatter replies 'Not the same thing a bit!' In trying to contain meaning, Alice in fact sets in motion a chain of proliferating, uncontrollable meanings. Meanings cannot be contained: by its very nature meaning is always liable to run off in some other direction than that to which it is supposedly dedicated and held in place. Again, the literary text may exploit this self-consciously so that ambiguity or even more complex levels of meaning feature explicitly in the text. Derrida has a special interest in Joyce's writing, and in sections of *Ulysses* and in *Finnegan's Wake* (1939) in particular the latent energy in language seems to be released as far as is imaginable. The endless slipping and sliding of language and meaning in the latter is a release of the full play of signification normally controlled and repressed in conventional discourse, as if the latent energy in the atoms of linguistic particles had been discovered. The range of associations generated by one sentence gives some indication of this, especially if we take the opening and closing lines of the novel which come together to form a syntactical unit and hence a cyclical pattern suggesting that there is no end to the permutations of meaning to be engendered in language and conscious-ness as the text runs endlessly on where, with apologies to T.S. Eliot, in the beginning is the end and in the end the beginning:

> riverrun, past Eve and Adam's, from swerve of shore to bend of bay, brings us by a commodius vicus of recirculation back to Howth Castle and environs.

> A way a lone a last a loved a long the

Such a view of language raises significant questions about the nature of criticism and interpretation. The idea of finding a correct, definitive interpretation is undermined in two ways. First because the language which makes up a text is never complete or contained but always spilling over into different meanings: it is liable to *dissemination* however much institutions may try to limit and fix the ways in which a text can be read. Secondly, the language of criticism or interpretation is itself subject to the conditions of *diffarence*, and the more it attempts a particular *closure,* the more other meanings which are excluded demand to be heard. In other words, there can be no wrong readings or interpretations: as the American deconstructionist Paul de Man has said, 'All reading is misreading'. Language by its very nature is meaningful. What is in contention is the meanings which are legiti-mated – those which come to be accepted and those which are excluded. Henry James's short story, 'The Figure in the Carpet' (1909) can be read as a comment on the impulse to find *the* definitive, ultimate meaning or explanation in a text, and has been adopted by decon-structionist critics as a kind of exemplum in this respect.[9] In the story a young critic is told by a novelist, Vereker, whose works he greatly admires but feels along with other readers he never fully understands, that there is a definitive figure or pattern concealed in his novels. However Vereker dies before he imparts the secret, and so the supposed final explanation remains elusive – or deferred. The tale has been read in different ways, as with many of James's short stories. It has been seen as a key to James's fiction, and indeed interpreting literary texts generally, in that they are often thought of as possessing an absolute meaning or kernel of truth. Conversely, it has been seen as an enactment of Derrida's notion of deferment – that complete meaning always escapes. The very debate about this text seems to be a comment on the nature of interpretation: that texts of any kind, especially literary texts, cannot be held in place in a fixed system of knowledge and contain a finite, absolute meaning.

'Depth' and 'surface' readings

In Joseph Conrad's *Heart of Darkness*, the anonymous narrator who introduces the character of Marlow provides the reader with some advice, a reading strategy for Marlow's tale which is, as I have suggested earlier, a complex narrative. Like 'The Figure in the Carpet', it does not offer an apparently clear and singular meaning:

> The yarns of seamen have a direct simplicity, the whole meaning of which lies within the shell of a cracked nut. But Marlow was not typical (if his propensity to spin yarns be excepted), and to him the meaning of an episode was not inside like a kernel but outside, enveloping the tale which brought it out only as a glow brings out a haze, in the likeness of one of these misty halos that sometimes are made visible by the spectral illumination of moonshine.[10]

The narrator's view of Marlow's narrative here – and presumably Conrad's – is an attempt to shift the reader from the preconception that texts contain a central core of meaning to which they can be reduced, or that below the surface we will find the 'truth' contained in the tale. Now certainly many literary texts might be thought of as revealing a central meaning and literary criticism has, more often than not, colluded in this. It is quite hard to read *Mansfield Park* as a plural, open text; its structure seems to work centripetally so that plot, action, character and language work to produce a centralized core of values focused on *Mansfield Park*. In *Heart of Darkness* though we are invited to range more freely over the surface of the text and not to organize, or organiscize it into a neat 'kernel' of meaning. These different ways of reading can be thought of as either reinforcing the 'logocentrism' of discourse, or an attempt to break from it. Ultimately language will still produce centralized forms of meaning rather like a magnetic force field, but a range of alternative meanings may come into play which can displace the singular, orthodox approach which, far from allowing literature to function as a liberating experience, imposes boundaries and restrictions on how meaning can circulate. Perhaps the mistake we make, and which language encourages us to make, is that in accepting the 'kernel' or 'depth' model of reading, we do not recognize that these meanings are themselves signs or language, another text to be deciphered. As Professor Morris Zapp, a character in David Lodge's novel *Small World* (1984) says: 'To understand a message is to decode it. Language is a code. *But every decoding is another encoding*'. To claim to find meaning behind or beyond language is to claim a kind of metaphysical knowledge, to invest language with powers which claim a higher authority than the materiality of the sign itself.

Literature and history

Another kind of language which claims a sort of 'presence' beyond its textuality, indeed which more often than not conceals its nature as language and text, is historical writing. There are many different kinds of historical writing, or writing which comes to be thought of as historical in some way or other, and I do not propose to attempt any classification of them here. But most historical discourse does lay claim to a sense of 'pastness', to a past time which has existed and is independent of the language used to describe it; the past is usually thought of as reflected through the language rather than constructed by it. In this respect, historical writing is very much involved with ascertaining facts, motives and explanations, and establishing forms of historical 'truth'. Such writing is centred on the past and its components, and we might well apply the 'kernel' metaphor to the way it works and is read. I want to consider the kinds of relations which have existed between English and History as disciplines and the ways in which these relations have been questioned and rethought. This is relevant for several reasons. I have referred to 'history' quite often in this book in various senses, but it has not been interrogated or problematized as a form of knowledge or discourse in the way that literature and literary criticism have. English and History have often been thought of as complementary subjects or disciplines, and although usually conceived of as different in various ways from literature – in terms of 'fact' and 'fiction' for example – an understanding of history is often thought of as helpful in forming a 'background' against which literary works can be studied. Some historians would also see literature as having an historical use, either as primary text material, or in giving a sense of historical atmosphere and offering an imaginative extension to the conventionally considered more factual and objective discipline of History. But in other ways English and History seem to share very little; the ways of reading are quite different for example. In whatever ways, literary study and criticism usually examine the linguistic properties of texts, but students of History would not be concerned with the text as a *text* in the same way. The kinds of conventions governing the subjects are quite distinct: English suggests imagination, fiction, sensibility or feeling; History objective, scientific investigation. Historical events are believed to be observable whereas literary ones are invented.

At a theoretical level, until recently there has been little interchange. Philosophy of History has been largely concerned with ways of knowing the past, and literary theory directed at a particular kind of writing or discourse. However, the American historian Hayden White has broken with disciplinary conventions and applied elements of literary theory to historical texts. His argument is that history and fiction have much in common, employing narrative devices and systems of rhetoric to construct a verbal image of 'reality': 'viewed simply as verbal artefacts histories and novels are indistinguishable from one another'.[11] He suggests that what distinguishes the literary from the historical is not fiction versus fact, but different textual properties. Literary and historical texts should thus be viewed as forms of writing and not mutually exclusive in terms of their supposed respective qualities of imagination and fact.

This reworking of History is helpful in relation to intertextuality. Historical 'background' becomes itself a form of text which we may use to align with a literary text, but we need to be as aware of how the meanings produced through what we call History are themselves constructions which we then employ to understand other artefacts. By applying literary theory to historical writing History is not undermined, rather we can see how it functions as a form of knowledge. There is no reason why we should stick rigidly to traditional discipline boundaries: traditional interdisciplinary study has meant studying one subject alongside another, but it now seems feasible to go beyond these apparently conventional but arguably arbitrary separations. By studying *writing* rather than the separate categories of English, History, Philosophy, Popular Culture and so on, possibilities arise that were hitherto precluded for a much broader conception of 'text' which transcends what all too frequently becomes a narrow institutional activity. In much the same way, I have already suggested, literary theory can be applied to the discourse of psychoanalysis as well as the more conventional reverse activity. This raises issues which go beyond literary theory and the study of literary texts, but perhaps is no bad thing. If literary, and other forms of theory lead to the redefinition, or collapse, of established fields of knowledge and associated ways of thinking, then change and progress are possible. Whether this is desirable depends on whether we think an understanding of how a literary culture comes into being, and how judgements about value, quality and truth are produced, is valuable. It also raises the question of whether we wish knowledge to remain in specific disciplines, or to examine wider issues about the relationships of what appear to be distinct areas to each other.

To offer a conclusion to this – or perhaps an opening – with an analogy: if we think of the various fields of knowledge as being like a galaxy of stars, then connections can be made between them. According to scientific laws, they are held in place by a series of force fields, and their motions and orbits are thus inextricably linked and interdependent. It would be impossible to chart all these forces and movements: it is more than any one person or society could do. But we can recognize the principles underlying these phenomena; in the same way texts, subjects or disciplines, and forms of knowledge might be seen to function. Literature is part of a much larger system which holds in place certain kinds of knowledge, and is held in place in turn by other kinds of knowledge. Working within such a framework may well produce new kinds of writing or discourse. There are some recent writers whom it would be impossible to classify as critics, theorists, autobiographers or creative. The French writer, Hélène Cixous, or British writers such as Bernard Sharratt and Carolyn Steedman[12] have started to break down the conventions of particular modes of writing to produce challenging texts which clearly owe much to theoretical approaches, but also involve other kinds of language from diverse areas. If one result of participating in a theoretical approach is to allow us to view literature differently, abandoning the comfortable insularity of 'English' for an uncomfortable, less familiar but arguably more productive relationship to all kinds of writing, then certainly we will not be inactive or passive readers.

A note on structuralism and poststructuralism

Structuralism and *poststructuralism* are terms which are used quite frequently with reference to literary theory, although they also apply to much wider fields of study and knowledge, from Cultural Studies and film to architecture and anthropology. Like most umbrella terms, they tend to be used in rather different ways, and as with modernism and postmodernism as we shall see, it is difficult to determine precisely where the boundary between the two categories is drawn. With regard to the material covered in this book so far, some theoretical approaches could be viewed as clearly more structuralist in character and others more poststructuralist, and some not falling clearly into either area. I have on the whole avoided identifying theories as being structuralist or poststructuralist because it might imply a simple division or polarity in either chronological or methodological ways which is not always the case.

Structuralism stems largely from the work of Ferdinand de Saussure; the key features of his theory of language have already been discussed. The main flourishing of structuralism though occurred rather later, in the 1950s and for the next two decades; the main figures associated with the movement were French although arguably figures associated with Russian Formalism and the subsequent Prague Linguistic Circle, such as Roman Jakobson, also contributed to its development.

The French anthropologist Claude Lévi-Strauss drew on the work of Saussure to interpret the underlying foundations of what he saw as primitive societies, concentrating on activities such as dress, etiquette and the preparation of food – one of his major pieces is entitled 'The Raw and the Cooked'.[13] In a sense, Lévi-Strauss was applying Saussure's distinction between *parole* and *langue* in language to a much wider field of human activity, trying to establish that particular instances of behaviour or myths were manifestations of a universal underlying structure. He saw common structures inhering in myths, mainly binary oppositions, which become the fundamental way in which meaning is constructed, through similarity or difference. Hence, according to this view, a society and its culture can be reduced to various oppositional components, both abstract and concrete, such as good/bad, man/woman, parent/child, white/black, and so on. Lévi-Strauss epitomizes the main characteristic of structuralism in its preoccupation with structures or systems and classification.

Roland Barthes, whose theory of narrative we have already considered, is also usually seen as central to the high period of modern

European structuralism; the distinction he makes in narrative between the units of function of 'catalysers' and 'nuclei' is an example, and much narrative theory from Propp to Genette can be viewed as structuralist in its methodology. The key work by Barthes here though is *Mythologies* (1957) in which he too uses Saussure's linguistic model to explore and analyse an eclectic range of objects and images in contemporary French popular culture. These range from soap powder and wrestling to toys and the latest model of Citroen. The volume also contains the essay 'Myth Today', in which Barthes develops Saussure's theory of the sign (*signifier + signified*) which he calls a form of 'primary signification' into a second level of signification. This 'secondary signification' arises from the sign produced at the primary level, where the signified in turn becomes a secondary signifier suggesting a meaning beyond its literal one; for Barthes this is the level at which 'myth' arises. An example of this from the realm of popular culture would be the set of signifiers which produce the signified of a brand of soap powder, but the soap powder in turn signifies qualities of whiteness, healthiness, purity and prestige. The power of an advertisement working in this way lies in the secondary signification's connotations – the myths which are brought into play. An example of this kind of analysis applied to a literary text is the use of images of objects in E.M. Forster's *Howards End* (1910) such as the house Howards End, or the Wych Elm in its garden, which acquire meanings and values of continuity, pastness and English rurality which transcend their literal materiality. Barthes' aims are not of course purely analytical; he states that semiology is 'a science of forms', but also that it deals with 'values'. Semiology does not, he argues, evacuate history from the process of analysis, but rather it involves and addresses history: ' ... the more a system is specifically defined in its forms, the more amenable it is to historical criticism. ... a little formalism turns one away from history, but a lot brings one back to it'. Barthes' target in *Mythologies* is what he calls the 'bourgeois norm', and he reveals a series of myths which underpin or position viewers and readers who he sees as composing the French bourgeoisie or middle classes.

Structuralism might seem at times to be rather schematic, and Terry Eagleton has parodied the most mechanical kinds of structuralist approach in *Literary Theory:*

Suppose we are analyzing a story in which a boy leaves home after quarrelling with his father, sets out on a walk through the forest in the heat of the day and falls down a deep pit. The father comes out in search of his son, peers down the pit, but is unable to see him because of the darkness. At that moment the sun has risen to a point directly overhead, illuminates the pit's depths with its rays and allows the father to rescue his child. After a joyous reconciliation, they return home together. . . .

. . . What the structuralist critic would do would be to schematize the story in diagrammatic form. The first unit of signification, 'boy quarrels with father', might be rewritten as 'low rebels against high'. The boy's walk through the forest is a movement along a horizontal axis, in contrast to the vertical axis 'low/high', and could be indexed as 'middle'. The fall into the pit 'a place below ground' signifies 'low' again, and the zenith of the sun 'high'. The reconciliation between father and son restores an equilibrium between 'low' and 'high', and the walk back home together, signifying 'middle', marks this achievement of a suitably intermediate state. Flushed with triumph, the structuralist rearranges his rulers and reaches for the next story.[14]

Although Eagleton's parody is aimed at earlier structuralist critics than Barthes, it does point to the potential for a reductionist mode of interpretation which emphasizes form at the expense of content and context. However, the two key changes which structuralism was instrumental in effecting in critical practice were, first a *decentring of the subject*: that is, individual subjects were seen as marginal to and effects of signifying systems rather than controlling them, and second, the methodology was undiscriminating and universally applicable so that advertisements or comics could be analysed alongside classic literary texts – popular culture was as valid an object of study as high culture and thus the established critical hierarchy could be challenged.

Poststructuralism

Poststructuralism, as its name suggests, can be viewed generally as a development from structuralism, though the two movements do overlap and share several common areas; indeed some theorists such as Roland Barthes or Jacques Lacan can be seen as having both structuralist and poststructuralist phases or dimensions in their work. The sections in this book dealing with deconstruction and Derrida's notion of logocentrism, and on discourse and Foucault's theories on power and knowledge, together with theories of textuality following the death of the author, are aspects of poststructuralism. One of the central tenets of poststructuralism is that whereas structuralism emphasized the underlying structures of meaning in a fairly secure, foundational way, meaning in poststructuralism is always temporary and in a state of flux, never stabilized or rooted in any way; Derrida's

concept of différance implies this. Barthes' theory of secondary signification anticipates the indefinite chains of meaning where signifieds
in their turn become new signifiers, and so on. A text is also caught up
in a network of intertextuality; it may temporarily acquire a particular
meaning as a reader interprets or 'activates' it, but this is never more
than a particular and relational meaning as a text is caught up in new
and different cultural webs. If we take a poem such as Wallace
Stevens, *'Anecdote of the Jar'*:

> I placed a jar in Tennessee,
> And round it was, upon a hill.
> It made the slovenly wilderness
> Surround that hill.
>
> The wilderness rose up to it,
> And sprawled around, no longer wild.
> The jar was round upon the ground
> And tall and of a port in air.
>
> It took dominion everywhere.
> The jar was gray and bare.
> It did not give of bird or bush,
> Like nothing else in Tennessee.

This poem foregrounds the problematics of interpretation, and resists
any attempts to have a definitive interpretation imposed on it; in this it
provides a model for the elusiveness of meaning more generally in any
text. Its signifiers produce signifieds which in turn suggests further
possibilities of meaning – the play between signifier and signified
becomes seemingly endless rather than a fixed relationship. Words
which in 'normal' contexts would provide little difficulty such as 'port'
or 'give' – become opaque; any overall meaning in the poem is only
glimpsed temporarily, if at all. (I have though heard one ingenious
interpretation of this poem, as an allegory for the illicit distillation of
'moonshine' – by an eminent professor!) From a structuralist point of
view, the poem also lends itself to illuminating analysis; there are
several possible binary oppositions, and the phonetic patterning is also
revealing with strong rhymes at certain points, but an absence of
rhyming symmetry where one might expect or desire a rhyme to be;
syntactically there are interesting structures as well. In fact, Stevens'
poem provides a very helpful text not only to illustrate aspects of
structuralist and poststructuralist approaches, but several of the theories dealt with earlier with respect to literary language, in particular
Shklovsky's concept of *defamiliarization* and Bakhtin's identification

of *centripetal* as opposed to *centrifugal* texts. Several of the theories associated with Russian Formalism can be linked to poststructuralism's abandonment of centralized meaning and authority, and also anticipate features of postmodernist writing as we shall see.

New historicism

One of the main outcomes of poststructuralist theory and its emphasis on deconstruction was the emergence of a group of theorists and critics who developed a methodology for reading texts in relation to history; their emphasis on the past is very much bound up with textuality but moves away from the formalist aspects of structuralism and poststructuralism. *New historicism* aims to study literature in its historical context, and in this respect might superficially not seem to be far removed from some examples of English literary criticism such as John Dover Wilson's *Life in Shakespeare's England* (1911) or E.M.W. Tillyard's *The Elizabethan World Picture* (1943) which present Shakespeare's plays in relation to what is taken as their historical 'background'. The English Renaissance period in particular has been represented in English culture as a period of relative harmony combined with great artistic richness and economic expansion, what has been called 'The Golden Age', and Shakespeare's plays have been read as an expression of these themes and placed in this organicized view or construction of the past.

New historicism and related critical work have been especially productive in rethinking or deconstructing the kinds of assumptions made about the past and literature's place in it, particularly with regard to Shakespeare and the Elizabethan period. The perceived celebration of the individual human subject in the Renaissance, where the idea of 'Man' at the centre of nature is constituted and from which stems the driving force of humanism, also made the literature of this period and the critical responses that reinforced such a view an ideal object of study for the application of theories which view 'Man', power, knowledge and history in very different ways. *New historicism* then proposes a new, or alternative history to the conventional, established historical accounts and practice through which literary texts had been largely studied. This is achieved by turning away from an apparently stable, fixed history which formed a kind of backcloth to the imaginative workings of the artist's mind, to a past which was uneven, fragmented, even unfinished so that history is a site of conflict which is ongoing, not a stable form of containment. In contrast, the idea of a unified world view which has proved so powerful in the historical representation and cultural reception of the Elizabethan period, limited and determined the kind of response to literary texts from the period, for example Tillyard's view of Caliban in *The Tempest* (1611):

> The whole play is alive with the sense of creation's flux and not blind to creation's limit. Caliban may hover between man and beast, yet in the end he shows himself incapable of the human power of education. Prospero too learns his own lesson. He cannot transcend the terms of his humanity. In the end he acknowledges Caliban, 'this thing of darkness, mine': man for all his striving towards the angels can never be quit utterly of the bestial, of the Caliban, within him.[15]

The kind of world view in which the play is placed to generate this reading tends towards a universal, non-specific and metaphysical conception which it is assumed is common to all 'men'; it ignores specificities such as class, gender, race, and the possibilities of political dissent and other forms of order and disorder. This kind of historical view can be extended to provide a map or graph-like image of the progression of English literature in historical terms which represents the past as relatively straightforward and unproblematic. Tillyard views the Renaissance in relation to the Victorian period in ways which simplify the past and consciousness:

> one of the things that most separates the Elizabethan from the Victorian world. In the latter there was a general pressure of opinion in favour of the doctrine of progress: the pessimists were in opposition. In the Elizabethan world there was an equal pressure on both sides, and the same person could be simultaneously aware of each.[16]

L.C. Knights in *Drama and Society in the Age of Jonson* (1937) uses a similar historical contrast in talking about 'being brought up on nineteenth-century conceptions of "natural equality" as opposed to the 'sixteenth-century conception of degree'.[17] Knights does in fact anticipate one of the features of new historicism in drawing attention to his own historical position; for a new historicist critic, the study of the past cannot be objective and the present transcended, it is constructed from and determined by the range of textual materials available. This has meant that some new historicists have turned to texts that would not be traditionally included in any literary canon; this has sometimes coincided with feminist and postcolonial theories as we shall see shortly. One of the main exponents of new historicism is the American critic Stephen Greenblatt, whose *Renaissance*

Self-Fashioning (1980) examines the question of subjectivity in Elizabethan literature, and the extent to which an individual was able to create an identity free from surrounding social forces. In the chapter dealing with the plays of Christopher Marlowe, Greenblatt opens the discussion by considering the account of a merchant, John Scarroll, on board a boat which sailed to the West African coast in 1586, whose landing party wantonly destroyed the town which they entered. He relates the account of this incident to the contemporaneous production of *Tamburlaine the Great* (1587) and proceeds to consider the play not in terms of its literary conventions but the 'acquisitive energies of English merchants, entrepreneurs, and adventurers, promoters alike of trading companies and theatrical companies'. The mechanics of rampaging and ruthless economic expansionism are paralleled in the character of Tamburlaine, 'a desiring machine that produces violence and death'.

New historicism is most strongly identified with an American group of critics, but it also has its British counterparts, although they are more usually referred to as *'cultural materialists'*. As well as the influence of Foucault in common with American new historicists, *cultural materialism* also develops out of the different Marxist approaches in the works of Raymond Williams and Louis Althusser. Foucault's emphasis is on the subjection of the individual, who is positioned by the dominant discourses of a particular historical moment, although he does acknowledge the possibility of resistance. Williams recognizes the force of economic determinism, but also sees the possibility of resistance and change; Althusser views culture as 'material' in the sense that culture is a part of the physical fabric of our lived experience, as theatrical performance, books and print, and has a tangible effect on our material conditions of existence. Catherine Belsey discusses *Arden of Faversham* (1592) in *The Subject of Tragedy: Identity and Difference in Renaissance Drama* (1985) with close reference to sixteenth-century accounts of Alice Arden's crime committed in 1551 of procuring and witnessing the murder of her husband. Belsey's thesis in the book is that although the individual humanist subject was in contention in late sixteenth-century drama, it is not fully stabilized as an ideological norm until the seventeenth century; in Renaissance tragedy the individual 'subject' constitutes the 'subject' of dramatic interest. In the case of *Arden of Faversham*, she argues that in the dominant discourse of patriarchy, the narrative of Alice Arden resists containment – her crime in fact was to 'defy the meaning of marriage ... to reopen the questions of sexual difference and thus the meaning of what it is to be a woman'.

An example of a new historicist or cultural materialist approach which embraces a wide range of textual and historical material is Peter Stallybrass and Allon White's *The Politics and Poetics of Transgression* (1986), which explores the construction of forms of low culture in parallel with the rise of the bourgeois or middle classes. They argue that aspects of what subsequently became viewed as vulgar or common life by the eighteenth and nineteenth centuries had a recognized and integrated function in medieval and Renaissance culture along the lines of Bakhtin's theory of the carnivalesque. The growth of the middle classes and bourgeois sensibility were defined increasingly against the 'Other' which constituted various forms of unacceptable and contaminating social and discursive formations ranging from the sewer and excretory bodily functions to the fairground. Stallylbrass and White draw on psychological theories from Freud and Kristeva as well as Marxist, Foucauldian and Bakhtinian theories and the book demonstrates the possibilities of theoretical argument when applied to a diverse range of primary material. Their starting point for defining 'Otherness' is Edward Said's theory of Orientalism: 'European culture gained in strength and identity by setting itself off against the Orient as a sort of ... underground self.[18]

Postcolonial theory

Edward Said's *Orientalism* (1978) identifies 'the systematic discipline' of western colonial discourse on the Orient as a means of political control: 'Orientalism can be discussed and analysed as the corporate institution for dealing with the Orient ... as a Western style for dominating, restructuring and having authority over the Orient.'[19] Said applies Foucault's theory of discourse and 'truth-knowledge-power' to the wide-ranging forms of writing representing the Orient as a means of acquiring and maintaining colonial control. As with most theoretical categories, postcolonialism covers a wide and diverse range of writing, and certainly there had been critiques of imperialist culture before Said; Frantz Fanon's *The Wretched of the Earth* (1961) examined the ways in which colonialism rewrites a nation's past as well as its present: 'Colonialism is not satisfied merely with hiding people in its grip and emptying the native's brain of all form and content. By a kind of perverted logic, it turns to the past of the oppressed people, and distorts, disfigures and destroys it.' [20] Poststructuralist theories, with their emphases on deconstruction and decentring, have informed the rise of postcolonial theory and this has highlighted further the ethnocentricity of European literature, and in particular the 'English-ness' of English literature. Said argues that not only was Orientalism a system of control, but also that it allowed the colonialists to reinforce their own position, to consolidate their own identity. The discourse of Orientalism circulated narratives about cruelty, sensuality, despotism, laziness and so on which constitute the negative 'Other' against which a positive identity could be constructed; Said and other postcolonial critics are at pains to point out that this discourse is still with us if in mutated forms, as is the (post)colonial project – recent interventions in the Gulf or the Falklands employ narratives which legitimate such imperialist activity; in *Culture and Imperialism* (1993) Said states, 'Narrative itself is the representation of power, and its teleology is associated with the global role of the West'.

Said links Orientalism to Gramsci's concept of hegemony; he draws on Gramsci's distinction between the 'civil' and the 'political' society, the former being composed of 'non-coercive' units such as the family, schools, unions, and the latter being state institutions such as the militia and police. As Gramsci argued, culture operates largely in the civil domain, and by consent rather than domination. Orientalism is thus all the more effective because it works by consensus, in juxtapos-ing the Occidental norm of 'us' against the Oriental Other of 'them'. This consensual identification can be seen to resonate across a diverse range of texts, from popular writing such as *The Boy's Own Paper* adventure stories (a particularly good example is Major T. Gorham's 'Falcons of the Frontier' in *The Boy's Own Paper* (1925), for its illustrations as well as narrative), to travel writing, documentaries, autobiographies and high literature. Although the literary character-istics might be quite different, the representations of non-European culture and colonized peoples tend to share similar characteristics when viewed from a Western perspective. Examples of canonical literary texts which have been reread in the light of postcolonial theory are Joseph Conrad's *Heart of Darkness* and E.M. Forster's *A Passage to India* (1924). Chinua Achebe has attacked Conrad's representation of Africa and Africans in an essay 'An Image of Africa: Racism in Conrad's *Heart of Darkness*' (1977). He attacks Conrad for both the generalized portrayal of Africa and Africans as an ugly, indistinguish-able frenzied mass in an early description, then for the more specific portrayal of an individual – the fireman on the steamer on which they are sailing into the jungle, 'who is not just limbs or rolling eyes'. Achebe criticizes the portrayal of the fireman, suggesting that Con-rad's positioning of him reinforces racial stereotypes and Eurocentric superiority: 'For Conrad, things (and persons) being in their place is of the utmost importance'. Conrad's description presented through Marlow of the individual fireman emphasizes individual physical characteristics rather than a complete persona, 'his pate shaved into queer patterns', 'filed teeth', 'ornamental scars on each of his cheeks', 'a piece of polished bone, as big as a watch, stuck flatways through his lower lip'. Homi Bhabha in his essay which addresses the construction of the colonial subject, 'Of Mimicry and Man: The Ambivalence of Colonial Discourse' (1984) argues that the Western 'racist gaze' denies the possibility of a whole being, unlike the 'myth of the undifferentiated whole white body'; in this sense the fireman as colonial subject becomes a number of disembodied parts which in turn emphasize disfigurement and grotesqueness. Edward Said has also recognized the colonial discourses circulating in *Heart of Darkness*, but emphasizes Conrad's own 'dislocated subjectivity', suggesting that the self-consciously circular narrative and ironic detachment are not 'average unreflecting witnesses of European imperialism'. For Said, *Heart of Darkness* confronts the very mechanisms which construct the imperialist project, and Marlow and Kurtz are unable to transcend their historical position and stand outside the all enveloping darkness of colonialist discourse: there is no Other available to them than that constructed within Western versions of Africa and the Orient.

A Passage to India has occupied a central place in English literary studies for several decades, not least as a frequently set 'A' Level text. In some respects, it shares similar themes and structures with *Heart of Darkness:* the journey to a remote, incomprehensible destination which both texts invite the reader to interpret as a geographical metaphor for psychological and philosophical voyages; the relationship of western to colonized communities; the intricate use of literary form. Although much critical writing on *A Passage to India* has emphasized the significance of the Indian setting, it has tended to consider it more in terms of its symbolic function within the formal structure of the novel and to view it as an extension of western imagination, as a platform for the psycho-spiritual drama which many critics have seen as being the central meaning of the novel. Sara Suleri, in 'The Geography of *A Passage to India*' rejects this kind of approach:

> Thus geography is subsumed into the more immediate and familiar territory of the liberal imagination, in the act of recolonizing its vagrant subject with the intricacies of a defined sensibility.
>
> Such is the imagination, of course, that legitimizes a text like *A Passage to India* as a humanely liberal parable for imperialism, and allows a reader like

Trilling to interpret the novel's depiction of Eastern action as a metaphor for the behaviour of the West. In other words, the only difference of India inheres in the fact that it is symbolic of something the Western mind must learn about itself.[21]

Suleri though goes on to argue that in spite of the novel's susceptibility to such liberal Western readings, it can in fact be reread as a text which refuses 'even the European attempt to coax it into metaphoricity'. Forster 'transgresses Orientalist decorum by implying India is not really other at all, but merely a mode or passageway that constitutes a reading of the West'. It is in the inability to grasp the otherness of India, in particular the non-significance of the Marabar Caves, their non-reducibility to rational interpretation, the nothingness with which they answer all attempts to address and position them. Edward Said detects parallels with Conrad's representation of Africa, seeing India posing problems for the novel form which Forster cannot deal with, 'a locale frequently described as unapprehendible and too large'.[22]

An extension of postcolonial theories is the acknowledgement of what can now be called 'literatures in English' rather than English literature. There has been an unprecedented growth in 'New Writings', that is writing originating from former colonial countries, together with writings about these new writings of a critical and theoretical nature. Chinua Achebe and Wole Soyinka, both acknowledged creative writers, have also produced works of a critical/theoretical orientation, and it is perhaps significant that such 'New Writing' has not been so rigidly bound by the traditional conventions which separate critical from creative activity. Issues of race and national identity though should not be seen as exclusively Oriental, African or Third World in provenance; they relate to Britain, Europe and America as Homi Bhabha's anthology, *Nation and Narration* (1990) shows, or Paul Gilroy's *There Ain't No Black in the Union Jack: The Cultural Politics of Race and Nation* (1987).

Postmodernism

Postmodernism and its antecedent movement, *modernism* are problematic categories for a number of reasons. The distinction between *modernism* and *postmodernism* is itself rather blurred: it is difficult to define a clear boundary in chronological, aesthetic or political terms. Some theorists and critics would consider the two movements as closely linked, others as quite antithetical. What can be said about both movements is that they are international – they transcend any strong national identification; they embrace a wide range of creative activity from literature and painting to architecture and music – *postmodernism* going beyond the 'high' or 'fine' arts to include popular and consumer products; both are preoccupied with the formal properties of art, albeit in different ways; and both can be seen as reactions to twentieth-century industrialized and mechanized societies, again in different kinds of responses. To a considerable extent, postmodernism can be seen to define itself against modernism, or certainly to be defined against modernism by poststructuralist theorists and critics, and to share many of the theoretical preoccupations of poststructuralism. Another rather simplified way of viewing it is to see a developing relationship from realism to modernism to postmodernism: that is from a predominating concern with an apparent truthfulness or verisimilitude to an apparent reality, to a preoccupation with the forms in which a version of reality could be represented and a rejection of the conventions of realism, to an increasing conviction that it is not possible to represent reality at all – there is no sense of a unified or underlying reality. One quality ascribed to postmodernism by most of its theorists is that it is composed entirely of 'surface': there is no inner meaning or 'depth', simulation has taken over from any sense of the real, indeed has become reality whether it be a soap opera (the treatment of characters as though they were real people by the popular press) to the intricate metafictional narratives of writers like Jorge Luis Borges, John Barth and John Fowles. The collapse of conventional demarcations between fact and fiction, present and past, reality and artifice, has become an increasingly common manifestation in texts which range from traditional categories of high to popular culture. John Barth's epic novel *The Sot-Weed Factor* (1960) self-consciously appropriates and parodies eighteenth-century stylistic devices playing with the fictional and historical past, disguise and counterfeiting being central themes. Advertisements now employ similar techniques to 'authenticate' products, even though the means of authentication are usually blatantly fictions or parodies – the 'Phileas Fogg' products, named after a character in Jules Verne's *Around the World in Eighty Days* (1873), display letters from Phileas Fogg on his travels as he discovers various authentic products:

Veracruz 4 August

My Dearest Aunt Agatha,
I write to you from the historic seaport of Veracruz with the most amazing gastronomic revelation, a Tortilla chip that is more aromatic than hot, a judicious blend of gentle spices and sour cream, the perfect accompaniment to a pre-prandial glass of Mexican tequila.

Your affectionate and respectful nephew,
Phileas Fogg[23]

The fact that these products are manufactured in Consett, a former steel making town in north-east England, is virtually obscured and eclipsed by the appeal to a pseudo pastness which has much in common with the rise of a heritage culture in Britain which also evokes a sense of the past that has more to do with contemporary marketing and comfortable myths of the past than actual history.

Postmodernism has resulted in what Peter Brooker has called 'a mood or condition of radical indeterminacy',[24] an abandonment of what the two leading French postmodernist philosophers, Jean-Francois Lyotard and Jean Baudrillard, identify as the grand or master narratives which underpinned and informed representations of life; an example would be in George Eliot's *Middlemarch* an underlying faith in human progress which is common to most nineteenth-century novels. This is especially noticeable in postmodernist novels which engage with history; whereas the nineteenth-century historical novel purported to represent a stable, accessible and shared historical narrative, for example Honoré de Balzac's *Cousin Bette* (1847) or Leo Tolstoy's *War and Peace* (1869), recent novels such as Graham Swift's *Waterland* (1983) or Julian Barnes's *A History of the World in 10½ Chapters* (1989) offer fragmented, slippery, relative and incomplete accounts of historical events – or rather fictions.

As with poststructuralist theories of the subject, postmodernist writing views the unitary individual subject as an untenable category; as early as 1931 Virginia Woolf's novel *The Waves* problematizes the coherence of the central character:

> What am I? I ask. This? No, I am that. Especially now, when I have left a room, and people talking, and the stone flags ring out my solitary footsteps, and I behold the moon rising, sublimely, indifferently, over the ancient chapel – then it becomes clear that I am not one and simple, but complex and many.[25]

The term postmodernism does not come into general usage though in Britain and America until the postwar period, and it is in the 1980s that the most intense theorization and debate takes place – the 'moment' of postmodernism in the sense of the intersection of cultural, political and historical forces together with a heightened awareness of the movement. A literary text which announces this moment at the start of the decade is Umberto Eco's *The Name of the Rose*, which has been discussed already. Eco's multiple cultural roles, as critic, theorist, journalist and media figure are paralleled by the text's discursive complexity and playfulness – full of allusion and reference, parody and pastiche, it resists neat classification. This indeterminacy seems to be an increasing characteristic of much postmodernist writing; the later works of Roland Barthes for example combine a more personal, creative and playful Barthes with a more detached, rigorously theoretical Barthes. Lyotard and Baudrillard both contribute towards a collapsing of the traditional boundaries between high and popular culture, between fact and fiction, between imitation or representation and reality. Baudrillard's work turns to what he calls 'hyper-reality', that is a reality which is based on 'simulation', an imaginary image which in fact displaces or eclipses actuality. For Baudrillard, Disneyland is the epitome of *hyper-reality*: Disneyland is a perfect model of all the entangled orders of simulation. To begin with it is a play of illusions and phantasms: pirates, the frontier, the future world, etc. This imaginary world is supposed to be what makes the operation successful. But what draws the crowds is undoubtedly the much more social microcosm, the miniaturized religious revelling in *real* America, in its delights and drawbacks.[26]

Hyper-reality comes to include even the Gulf War which he proclaimed was not a real war, but a media war; undoubtedly the television images of the war were extraordinarily powerful and detailed but his denial of the material reality of the war beyond surface images has provoked strong criticism of the postmodernist vision of a world consisting only of the play of signs and ignoring or eclipsing lived experience. Lyotard's postmodernism is not quite so extreme, or at least has not proved as contentious. His critique of knowledge and truth in *The Postmodern Condition* (1979) was extremely influential, and was largely responsible for bringing the postmodernist debate into the public domain. In some respects, his attack on 'metanarratives', that is overarching narratives with a universalizing truth function, is not dissimilar to some of Foucault's theories. Lyotard's view of *metanarratives* is that they impose restrictive boundaries on an otherwise pluralist, diverse cultural formation; they serve to delimit discourses into recognized units and to exclude or marginalize voices which do not fit into the dominant groups. What interests Lyotard in scientific knowledge for example is not the truths or otherwise which science lays claim to, but the processes by which such truths have been validated and the cultural position which science has come to occupy since the Enlightenment. He argues that science increasingly is being seen not as a source of truth – indeed it has become more problematic since the Second World War with the implications of such discoveries as the splitting of the atom resulting in the atomic bomb, progress is not now seen so strongly as resulting in a definite and positive end. What Lyotard also sees, like Baudrillard, is a dissolution of history, a kind of *fin de siecle* entropy; in his essay 'The Year 2000 Has Already Happened' (1985) he draws on a number of theses to demonstrate that history has, or is about to end or implode, echoing the postmodernist historian Francis Fukuyama's pronouncement of 'the end of history'.

The combination of the demise of history and reality reduced to an endless play of signs or simulacra has not endeared itself to Marxist theorists any more than it has to traditional humanist critics. Fredric Jameson and Terry Eagleton have both responded to the rejection of Marxism that much postmodernist theory implies. Jameson's extended essay, 'Postmodernism, or The Cultural Logic of Late Capitalism' (1984) locates postmodernism within capitalist ideology and maintains a Marxist critique of a movement which most of its theorists considered to be beyond Marxism. For Jameson, although he concurs with much postmodernist theory involving pastiche and surface representations, 'a new kind of flatness or depthlessness', these mask an inner depth which is the perpetuation of capitalism in a late phase that utilizes the images and techniques ascribed to postmodernism. The postmodernist preoccupation with *fin de siecle* or 'inverted millenarianism' issues such as the end of history and just about everything else, he sees as a distraction from the continuation of capitalism in its multinational forms and its mutated ideological manifestations; postmodernism is, for Jameson, 'not a style but a cultural dominant'. The effectiveness of postmodernism is its all-pervasiveness and its ability to rapidly and endlessly reproduce itself across a range of cultural and consumer products – indeed the collapse of the distinction between these is itself an ideological function of 'commodification' so that images of Coca-cola bottles or Campbell's Soup Cans as art 'foreground ... commodity fetishism'. A further effect of postmodernism is incomprehension, it normalizes or validates our inability to 'map the great global multinational and decentred communicational network in which we find ourselves caught as individual subjects'. What Jameson calls 'real' history is lost and displaced by 'a history of aesthetic styles', a feature of what he calls 'schizophrenia' which he borrows from Lacan's use of the term to imply chaos in language, a breakdown of the normal relations between signifiers which 'fail to link up in a coherent sequence'. Eagleton also makes links between the ways in which postmodernism represents art and commodity products in 'Capitalism, Modernism and Postmodernism' (1985), using Marx's concept of 'commodity fetishism'; he views postmodernism as an extension of the way that Marx considers products to be given an identity and value separate from the labour which produces them which is the key to the alienation of labour and the exploitation of the working by the capitalist classes. Postmodernism in effect normalizes this fetishism, celebrates endlessly the products of late twentieth-century capitalist society.

There are though some examples of a more positive theorization of postmodernism, in particular from a feminist perspective. Patricia Waugh, in *Practising Postmodernism/Reading Postmodernism* (1992), demonstrates that the development of feminist theory coincides with the rise of postmodernism, especially from the 1970s onwards, although 'debates within feminism have tended to be ignored within discussions of Postmodernism and *vice versa*'. She argues though that several of the key theoretical elements of feminism are not far removed from those of postmodernism: the 'self-reflexive mode: questioning its own legitimating procedures in a manner which seems to bring it close to Postmodernism' is a feature of this tendency, even though there are significant differences. A crucial difference though is that whereas postmodernism postulates, and in some manifestations celebrates the decentred and fragmented subject, 'feminism needs coherent subjects but has found alternative ways of articulating them' which avoid the conventions of humanism or postmodernism. She goes on to argue that 'many women writers are using postmodern strategies of disruption to re-imagine the world in which we live, while resisting the nihilistic implications of the [postmodernist] theory', citing writers such as Angela Carter, Jeanette Winterson, Margaret Atwood, Maggie Gee and Fay Weldon as some examples. She believes that many feminist writers have succeeded in rethinking the self 'without abandoning subjectivity to dispersal and language games', whilst also not producing 'the failure of love and relationship' which is common to many texts by male modernist and postmodernist writers. Linda Hutcheon, in *The Politics of Postmodernism* (1989), also sees feminist writers and artists as developing some of the characteristics of postmodernism in ways which challenge the dominant representations of women; she examines how Angela Carter's short story 'Black Venus' which explores the relationship between Baudelaire and his mulatto mistress, Jeanne Duval, the history of male desire is 're-coded' so that the ' "colonized territory" of the female body ... is coded as erotic masculine fantasy, and then re-coded in terms of female experience'. Hutcheon countenances the possibility that 'postmodern strategies can be deployed by feminist artists to deconstructive ends – that is to begin to move towards change'; she considers parody to be an essential aspect of feminist postmodernism, a way of undermining and challenging male dominated narratives.

The relationship envisaged here between postmodernism and feminism can serve to remind us that we need to be mindful about the potential exclusivity of theoretical and critical categories; to read a text from one dominant theoretical perspective will inevitably marginalize or preclude other readings, and a radical interpretation which employs postcolonial theory for example may ignore issues of gender: we should be careful to avoid critical and theoretical exclusivity.

Notes

1 Florence Emily Hardy, *The Life of Thomas Hardy 1840–1928* (London, Macmillan, 1962), p. 218. First published in two volumes in 1928 and 1930.

2 Roland Barthes, 'Theory of the Text', in Robert Young, ed., *Untying the Text* (London, Routledge, 1981), p. 39.

3 Roland Barthes, 'Criticism as Language', in David Lodge, ed., *Twentieth-Century Literary Criticism* (London, Longman, 1972), p. 650. First published in 1963.

4 Antony Easthope, 'Literature, History, and the Materiality of the Text', *Literature and History*, Vol. 9:1, Spring 1983, p. 28.

5 Tony Bennett, 'Text, Readers, Reading Formations', *Literature and History*, Vol. 9:2, Autumn 1983, p. 216.

6 Michel Foucault, *The Archaeology of Knowledge* (London, Tavistock, 1972), p. 23. First published in France in 1969.

7 Jacques Derrida, 'Structure, Sign and Play in the Discourses of the Human Sciences', in *Writing and Difference* (London, Routledge, 1978), p. 278. First published in France in 1967.

8 Plato makes the point in *Phaedrus* (370 BC), through Socrates, about speech being more reliable than writing because of the presence of the speaker so his/her words are less likely to be misinterpreted – the written text is more open to interpretation. It is precisely for this reason that Jacques Derrida reverses this preference in an essay on Plato's *Phaedrus* where he argues against the myth of 'presence' and a single authoritative meaning, and stresses the importance of recognizing the multiple meanings or 'signifieds' of any text, which writing more readily allows through the absence of any apparent guarantor. See Plato, *Phaedrus*, translated by Walter Hamilton (Harmondsworth, Penguin, 1973), p. 101; and Jacques Derrida, 'Plato's Pharmacy', in *Disseminations*, translated by Barbara Johnson (Chicago, University of Chicago Press, 1981).

9 See the debate between J. Hillis Miller and Shlomith Rimmon-Kenan: J. Hillis Miller, 'The Figure in the Carpet' (1980); Shlomith Rimmon-Kenan,

'Deconstructive Reflections on Deconstruction; in Reply to Hillis Miller' (1980); and J. Hillis Miller, 'A Guest in the House; Reply to Shlomith Rimmon-Kenan's Reply' (1980). These are reprinted in Philip Rice and Patricia Waugh, eds., *Modern Literary Theory: A Reader* (London, Edward Arnold, 1989), pp. 172–93.

10 Joseph Conrad, *op. cit.*, p. 30.

11 Hayden White, 'The Fictions of Factual Representation', in Angus Fraser, ed., *The Literature of Fact* (New York, Columbia University Press, 1976), p. 22.

12 For examples of such innovative writings by these authors, see Hélène Cixous, 'The Laugh of Medusa' in Elaine Marks and Isabelle de Court-ivon, eds., *New French Feminisms* (Brighton, Harvester, 1980), pp. 245–64, first published in France in 1975; Bernard Sharratt, *Reading Relations: Structures of Literary Production: A Dialectical Text/Book* (Brighton, Harvester, 1982); and Carolyn Steedman, *Landscape for a Good Woman: A Story of Two Lives* (London, Virago, 1986).

13 Claude Lévi-Strauss, 'The Raw and the Cooked' in *Introduction to a Science of Mythology* (London, Jonathan Cape, 1978). First published in France in 1968.

14 Terry Eagleton, *Literary Theory: An Introduction* (Oxford, Blackwell, 1983), p. 95.

15 E.M.W. Tillyard, *The Elizabethan World Picture* (Harmondsworth, Penguin, 1963), p. 48. First published in 1943.

16 E.M.W. Tillyard, *op. cit.*, p. 34.

17 L.C. Knights, *Drama and Society in the Age of Jonson* (Harmondsworth, Penguin, 1962), p. 125. First published in 1937.

18 Edward Said, *Orientalism* (New York, Vintage Books, 1979), p. 7, quoted in Peter Stallybrass and Allon White, *The Politics and Poetics of Transgression* (London, Methuen, 1986), p. 5.

19 Edward W. Said, *op.cit.*, p. 3.

20 Frantz Fanon, *The Wretched of the Earth*, in Patrick Williams and Laura Chrisman, eds., *Colonial Discourse and Post-Colonial Theory: A Reader* (Hemel Hempstead, Harvester, 1993), p. 37.

21 Sara Suleri, 'The Geography of *A Passage to India*', in Dennis Walder, ed., *Literature in the Modern World* (Oxford, Oxford University Press, 1990), pp. 245–6.

22 Edward W. Said, *Culture and Imperialism* (London, Chatto & Windus, 1993), p. 243.

23 Taken from 'Phileas Fogg/Cool Tortilla' packet produced by Derwent Valley Foods Ltd, Consett, 1994.

24 Peter Brooker, 'Postmodern Postpoetry', in Antony Easthope and John Thompson, eds., *Contemporary Poetry Meets Modern Theory* (Hemel Hempstead, Harvester, 1991).

25 Virginia Woolf, *The Waves* (Harmondsworth, Penguin, 1951), p. 64. First
    published 1931.
26 Jean Baudrillard, 'Simulacra and Simulations', in Mark Poster, ed., *Jean
    Baudrillard: Selected Writings* (Cambridge, Polity Press, 1988), p. 171.

6 Further reading

The following are further introductory and more specialized texts which may be used to study in more detail some of the areas which have been introduced in this book. Those which are asterisked(*) are recommended for initial reading. Most of these works in turn will contain wider reading suggestions in their bibliographies and references.

Introductory and general works on literary theory

*Terry Eagleton, *Literary Theory: An Introduction* (Oxford, Basil Blackwell, 1983).
Peter Griffith, *Literary Theory and English Teaching* (Milton Keynes, Open University Press, 1987).
Jeremy Hawthorn, ed., *Criticism and Critical Theory* (London, Edward Arnold, 1984).
* Jeremy Hawthorn, *Unlocking the Text: Fundamental Issues in Literary Theory* (London, Edward Arnold, 1987).
Ann Jefferson and David Robey, eds., *Modern Literary Theory: A Comparative Introduction* Second Edition (London, Batsford, 1986).
Raman Selden, *Practising Theory and Reading Literature: An Introduction* (Hemel Hempstead, Harvester, 1989).
* Raman Selden and Peter Widdowson, *A Reader's Guide to Contemporary Literary Theory* Third Edition (Hemel Hempstead, Harvester, 1993).

General readers

These are helpful anthologies which contain selections of essays and extracts on various aspects of literary and critical theory.

David Lodge, ed., *Twentieth-Century Literary Criticism* (London, Longman, 1972).

David Lodge, ed., *Modern Criticism and Theory: A Reader* (Harlow, Longman, 1988).

K.M. Newton, ed., *Twentieth-Century Literary Theory: A Reader* (London, Macmillan, 1988).

Philip Rice and Patricia Waugh, *Modern Literary Theory: A Reader* (London, Edward Arnold, 1989).

Rick Rylance, ed., *Debating Texts: A Reader in Twentieth-Century Literary Theory and Method* (Milton Keynes, Open University Press, 1987).

Raman Selden, ed., *The Theory of Criticism From Plato to the Present: A Reader* (Harlow, Longman, 1988).

Douglas Tallack, ed., *Critical Theory: A Reader* (Hemel Hempstead, Harvester, 1995).

Reader and reception theory·

Umberto Eco, *The Role of the Reader: Explorations in the Semiotics of Texts* (Bloomington, Indiana University Press, 1979).

* Elizabeth Freund, *The Return of the Reader: Reader-Response Criticism* (London, Methuen, 1987).

Robert C. Holub, *Reception Theory: A Critical Introduction* (London, Methuen, 1984).

Wolfgang Iser, *The Act of Reading: A Theory of Aesthetic Response* (Baltimore, Johns Hopkins University Press, 1978).

Hans Robert Jauss, *Toward an Aesthetic of Reception* (Brighton, Harvester, 1982).

Language

Jonathan Culler, *Saussure* (London, Fontana, 1976).

Jonathan Culler, *Structuralist Poetics: Structuralism, Linguistics and the Study of Literature* (London, Routledge, 1975).

Roger Fowler, *Linguistic Criticism* (Oxford, Oxford University Press, 1986).

Roger Fowler, *Literature as Social Discourse: The Practice of Linguistic Criticism* (London, Batsford, 1981).

David Lodge, *The Modes of Modern Writing: Metaphor, Metonymy, and the Typology of Modern Literature* (London, Edward Arnold, 1977).

* Jeremy Tambling, *What is Literary Language?* (Milton Keynes, Open University Press, 1988).

Narrative

Peter Brooks, *Reading for the Plot: Design and Intention in Narrative* (Oxford, Oxford University Press, 1984).

Gérard Genette, *Narrative Discourse* (Oxford, Basil Blackwell, 1980).

Jeremy Hawthorn, ed., *Narrative: From Malory to Motion Pictures* (London, Edward Arnold, 1985).

Robert Scholes and Robert Kellogg, *The Nature of Narrative* (Oxford, Oxford University Press, 1966).

* Shlomith Rimmon-Kenan, *Narrative Fiction: Contemporary Poetics* (London, Methuen, 1983).

F.K. Stanzel, *A Theory of Narrative* (Cambridge, Cambridge University Press, 1984).

Ideology and Marxist theory

* Catherine Belsey, *Critical Practice* (London, Methuen, 1980).
* Tony Bennett, *Formalism and Marxism* (London, Methuen, 1979).
* Lennard J. Davis, *Resisting Novels: Ideology and Fiction* (London, Methuen, 1987).

Terry Eagleton, *Marxism and Literary Criticism* (London, Methuen, 1976).

John Frow, *Marxism and Literary History* (Oxford, Basil Blackwell, 1986).

Diane Macdonell, *Theories of Discourse: An Introduction* (Oxford, Blackwell, 1986).

Pierre Macherey, *A Theory of Literary Production* (London, Routledge, 1978).

Cliff Slaughter, *Marxism, Ideology and Literature* (London, Macmillan, 1980).

Raymond Williams, *Marxism and Literature* (Oxford, Oxford University Press, 1977).

Psychoanalytic theory

Colin MacCabe, *The Talking-Cure: Essays in Psychoanalysis and Language* (London, Macmillan, 1981).

Shlomith Rimmon-Kenan, *Discourse in Psychoanalysis and Literature* (London, Methuen, 1987).

* Elizabeth Wright, *Psychoanalytic Criticism: Theory in Practice* (London, Methuen, 1984).

Feminist theory

Mary Eagleton, ed., *Feminist Literary Theory: A Reader* (Oxford, Basil Blackwell, 1986).

Gayle Greene and Coppelia Kahn, *Making a Difference: Feminist Literary Criticism* (London, Methuen, 1985).

Juliet Mithchell, *Women: The Longest Revolution: Essays in Feminism, Literature and Psychoanalysis* (London, Virago, 1984).

* Toril Moi, *Sexual/Textual Politics: Feminist Literary Theory* (London, Methuen, 1985).

* Pam Morris, *Literature and Feminism: An Introduction* (Oxford, Blackwell, 1993).

K.K. Ruthven, *Feminist Literary Studies: An Introduction* (Cambridge, Cambridge University Press, 1984).

* Ruth Sherry, *Studying Women's Writing: An Introduction* (London, Edward Arnold, 1988).

Dale Spender, *Man Made Language* (London, Routledge, 1980).

Poststructuralism/deconstruction

Christopher Butler, *Interpretation, Deconstruction, and Ideology* (Oxford, Oxford University Press, 1984).

Jonathan Culler, *On Deconstruction: Theory and Criticism after Structuralism* (London, Routledge, 1983).

Richard Harland, *Superstructuralism: The Philosophy of Structuralism and Post-Structuralism* (London, Methuen, 1987).

* Christopher Norris, *Deconstruction: Theory and Practice* (London, Methuen, 1982).

Edward Said, *The World, the Text, and the Critic* (Cambridge, Mass., Harvard University Press, 1983).

Robert Young, ed., *Untying the Text: A Post-Structuralist Reader* (London, Routledge, 1981).

Postcolonial theory

Homi Bhabha, ed., *Nation and Narration* (London, Routledge, 1990).

Henry Louis Gates, Jr, ed., *Black Literature and Literary Theory* (London, Routledge, 1984).

Paul Gilroy, *There Ain't No Black in the Union Jack: The Cultural Politics of Race and Nation* (London, Hutchinson, 1987).

Edward W. Said, *Orientalism* (London, Routledge, 1978).

Edward W. Said, *Culture and Imperialism* (London, Chatto & Windus, 1993).

*Patrick Williams and Laura Chrisman, eds., *Colonial Discourse and Post-Colonial Theory: A Reader* (Hemel Hempstead, Harvester, 1993).

Postmodernism

Thomas Docherty, ed., *Postmodernism: A Reader* (Hemel Hempstead, Harvester, 1993).

Linda Hutcheon, *The Politics of Postmodernism* (London, Routledge, 1989).

Christopher Norris, *What's Wrong with Postmodernism: Critical Theory and the Ends of Philosophy* (Hemel Hempstead, Harvester, 1990).

*Madan Sarap, *An Introductory Guide to Post-Structuralism and Postmodernism* (Hemel Hempstead, Harvester, 1993).

*Patricia Waugh, ed., *Postmodernism: A Reader* (London, Edward Arnold, 1992).

Patricia Waugh, *Practising Postmodernism/Reading Modernism* (London, Edward Arnold, 1992).

Reference works

The following offer useful brief definitions of theoretical terminology.

Roger Fowler, ed., *A Dictionary of Modern Critical Terms: Revised and Enlarged Edition* (London, Routledge, 1987).

*Jeremy Hawthorn, *A Concise Glossary of Contemporary Literary Theory* (London, Edward Arnold, 1992).

Tim O'Sullivan, John Hartley, Danny Saunders, John Fiske, eds., *Key Concepts in Communication* (London, Methuen, 1983).

Index